Katharine
HEPBURN

Katharine HEPBURN

Jessica Hodge

Crescent Books
New York

Copyright © 1992 Brompton Books
Corporation

All rights reserved. No part of this
publication may be reproduced, stored in a
retrieval system or transmitted in any form
by any means, electronic, mechanical,
photocopying or otherwise, without first
obtaining the written permission of the
copyright owner.

This 1992 edition published by Crescent
Books,
distributed by Outlet Book Company, Inc.,
a Random House Company,
40 Engelhard Avenue,
Avenel, New Jersey 07001

Produced by
Brompton Books Corporation
15 Sherwood Place
Greenwich, CT 06830

ISBN 0-517-06706-4

8 7 6 5 4 3 2 1

Printed and bound in Hong Kong

Page 1: A studio shot of Hepburn in 1944, the year she
made *Dragon Seed*, based on Pearl S Buck's best-selling
novel, in which she plays a Chinese peasant girl. It is
one of her less convincing roles, though immensely
popular with wartime audiences.

Page 2: Kate still glamorous in the 1960s.

Right: Kate arrives back in Hollywood in November
1932. When her first film role in *A Bill of Divorcement*
was acclaimed by the critics, she was summoned back
from Europe, where she and husband Ludlow Ogden
Smith had gone in the hope of rescuing their failing
marriage.

Far right: Kate in the stage production of *The Warrior's
Husband* in 1930.

Contents

Chapter 1
FROM HARTFORD TO HOLLYWOOD
1907-1933

Fʀᴏᴍ her first arrival in Hollywood in 1932, aged 25 and with a Broadway hit already under her belt, Katharine Hepburn established herself as a unique presence. She was more interested in stage parts at the time and demanded, and was given, a huge fee; her screen debut, *A Bill of Divorcement,* was an instant hit. Brought up in an atmosphere of intellectual freedom and intense physical discipline, she was not prepared to tolerate the constraints of stardom. She refused to grant interviews, kept her private life to herself, and insisted on wearing loose-fitting slacks and sloppy sweaters rather than the tailored suits and low-cut dresses then regarded as the uniform of the female star. Her strong-minded, outspoken approach to her work had already got her into trouble with Broadway and summer stock producers, who were not used to being told how to do their jobs, and she had been fired from several productions. She had an equally abrasive effect on Hollywood, which did not know how to handle her. The combination of integrity and intelligence that she brought to screen roles was wholly new; with Hepburn, women in the cinema came of age.

Hepburn's career falls into several clearly definable phases. In the 1930s she made a number of successful and innovative films, and won her first Oscar for *Morning Glory* in 1933. By the late 1930s, however, a combination of dull, mainly costume, roles and her own brash and unco-operative personality led to a period of temporary eclipse. An apparently miraculous but actually well-orchestrated comeback with *The Philadelphia Story* was followed by a series of delightful comedies with Spencer Tracy, which also marked the beginning of a lasting private partnership. It is a measure of the unwilling respect Hepburn already inspired that this liaison never became gossip-column material.

Teamwork with Tracy did, however, place limitations on Hepburn's own development as

Opposite: This dramatic publicity shot was taken during the Broadway run of *The Philadelphia Story*, with which Kate made a triumphant comeback in 1939.

Below: Kate in Garboesque mood and barely recognizable in one of the standard studio shots required by RKO.

Right: Another early publicity shot taken on Kate's first arrival in Hollywood in 1932, this time looking vampish with that regular Hollywood prop, the cigarette. She was intensely impatient of Hollywood habits and the need to play at being a star. In her first confrontation with RKO's press department, she told them that her private life was her own and she did not believe in publicity. The studio did not for many months learn that she was married, and instead wild rumors abounded of a lesbian relationship with Laura Harding. The press soon scented the fact that a new star was rising on the set of RKO's latest picture, *A Bill of Divorcement*, however, and visiting reporters were delighted by Kate's appearance between takes in her ancient dungarees. RKO were much more disapproving and the offending garment was removed from her dressing room. Kate threatened to walk through the lot naked to retrieve them and when her bluff was called did indeed, as she later recalled, 'walk through the lot in my underpants.' The dungarees were returned but all pictures of the exploit were confiscated.

an actress. It was not until *The African Queen* in 1951 that she found a solo role worthy of her talents and embarked on a new phase both on screen and stage. The year 1952 found her on stage in London performing in George Bernard Shaw, 1955 saw her touring Australia in Shakespeare. Her swansong with Tracy was *Guess Who's Coming to Dinner*, which won her a second Oscar 34 years after the first, and after his death in 1967 she went on to star in two more Oscar-winning film roles and a musical, *Coco*. She finally emerged from her cocoon of privacy in the 1980s to write both about her relationship with Tracy and the making of *The African Queen*, which she regarded as a pivotal role, while in 1991 she reviewed her life in characteristically energetic and breathless style in her autobiography, *Me, Stories of My Life*, which ends with the two words 'Yes, lucky.'

The family into which Katharine Houghton Hepburn was born on November 8th, 1907 (not 1909 as some chroniclers have it), was no ordinary one. Both her parents were formidable, committed, independent-minded individuals. Dr Thomas Norval Hepburn, son of an Episcopalian minister, was a medical student when he first met Kit Houghton. Originally from Scotland, the Hepburns could trace their ancestry back to James Hepburn, Earl of Bothwell, third husband of Mary Queen of Scots. Tom Hepburn was a natural athlete, and physical fitness was a lifelong obsession which he passed on to his oldest daughter; he believed that a lazy body produced a lazy mind. A well-built, red-headed man with a booming Virginian voice, he was enough of an original that the strong-minded Kit Houghton said as soon as she met him: 'That's the one.'

Katharine Martha Houghton was a member of the rich and socially prominent Bostonian Houghton family. In 1892, when she was 13, her father committed suicide and her mother died soon after of cancer; the three Houghton sisters were subsequently supported by their maternal uncle. All three upstanding young women, they insisted, much to their uncle's shock, on attending Bryn Mawr, then regarded as the most academic of the women's colleges, and getting an education – Kit, as she was invariably known, with the stated intention of 'raising hell with established customs.' By the time she met Tom Hepburn she had already been to France with a girlfriend, sailing with a mere ten dollars in her pocket because her uncle disapproved and withheld her allowance.

Married in 1904, the Hepburns remained a devoted couple for nearly 50 years, until Kit's death in 1951. Their daughter has on many occasions been quoted as saying 'I don't believe in marriage . . . possibly the only happy marriage I've known was my parents'. They never argued about things . . . they only argued about ideas.' The Hepburns began their married life in Hartford, Connecticut, where Tom moved from an internship at the Hartford Hospital to a general surgical practice specializing in urology, then a very young science. As he prospered in his profession, Dr Hepburn was able to move his young family to more spacious and elegant accommodation, and Katharine – Kathy at first to her family, Red-

Left: Katharine Martha Hepburn, Kate's mother, with her two younger daughters Marion (center) and Margaret, arriving in London in 1935. Kate has written in her autobiography that from her mother she learnt: 'Don't give in. Fight for your future. *Independence* is the only solution. Women are as good as men. Onward!'

top to her father alone, who was delighted with his red-headed daughter – was born in a comfortable house on Hawthorne Street. Soon after her birth, Kit Hepburn, at the urging of her husband who felt that she needed more stimulation, attended a lecture by Emmeline Pankhurst, the British suffragette.

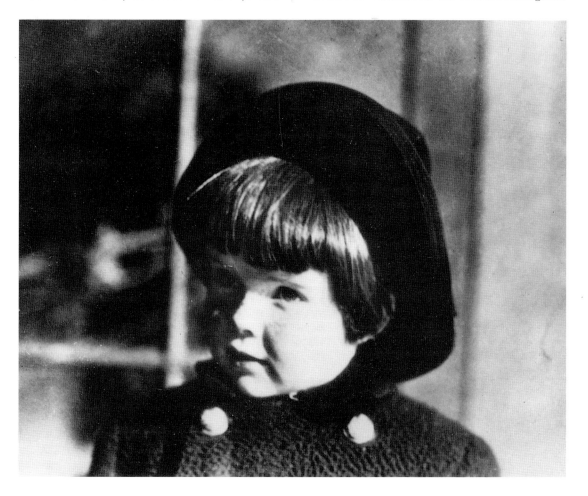

Left: Kate aged four. From her earliest years her father encouraged her to be a gymnast. She could stand and walk on her hands, turn handsprings and take a flying somersault off her father's shoulders. She writes 'I was standing on my head the other day and I got to thinking how probably unusual it is for someone of my age to do this.'

Above: Kate in 1921, the year after her brother's death. By this time she had left the girls' school she had been attending and was being tutored at home. The Hepburn family formed a self-contained unit, with Kate very much the older sister, but already young men were queuing at the Hepburn front door.

She became an ardent feminist and supporter of women's enfranchisement, taking the infant Kathy with her to suffragist meetings and lectures.

Four more children followed Kathy and her older brother Tom, and the Hepburn family regime was a spartan one, featuring cold baths, a bracing attitude to illness, and much competitive exercise. Kathy was encouraged to run, wrestle, box and climb trees with her one older and two younger brothers. In 1912 the family bought a part share in a summer cottage on the peninsula of Fenwick on the Connecticut shoreline, a popular retreat for the moneyed elite of Hartford, and here the Hepburn children were able to run even more wild in idyllic surroundings. Intellectually their upbringing was equally stimulating; whatever the topic of conversation in her parents' lively drawing room, from socialism and Marxism to

prostitution and venereal disease, the Hepburn children were never asked to leave but rather were encouraged to express their own opinions.

The first real upset in what seems like an ideal if bracing childhood came in 1920, when Kathy was 13, just the same age at which her mother was orphaned. She and her brother Tom were taken by their mother to New York to stay with her old Bryn Mawr friend Mary Towle, Kit's companion on her French escapade and now a successful lawyer. Staying a few extra days on their own, Tom and Kathy saw the movie *A Connecticut Yankee at King Arthur's Court*, based on the Mark Twain novel. On the morning that they were due to return to Hartford, Tom slept late and Kathy went upstairs to wake him. She found him hanging from a noose made from a curtain tie; he was quite dead but Kathy was still holding her brother's whole weight when medical help arrived 20 minutes later. The death was reported as suicide, although the Hepburn family believed it to be a tragic accident, the result of a midnight attempt by Tom, perhaps inspired by the hanging scene in the Twain film, to repeat a hanging trick he had once performed. Whatever the truth, the tragedy had a devastating effect on the young Kathy. She was drawn closer to her parents and also took much of the responsibility for her four younger siblings, while Kit Hepburn crusaded for the liberalization of birth-control legislation. But her schoolwork suffered, and the day school to which she had been sent, where she had failed to make any close friends, became increasingly uncongenial. Finally her parents agreed that she should be tutored at home.

Amateur dramatics had been a major part of life at Fenwick even before Tom's death, and afterward it seemed to provide Kathy with an essential outlet. In the summer of 1920 the local children under her direction put on backyard productions of *Bluebeard* and *Beauty and the Beast*. She also became an enthusiastic movie fan and an even keener sportswoman than before – crack tennis player, bronze-medal-winning figure skater, and one of the most promising young golfers in the country. This athleticism was to figure in several of her best films, notably *Pat and Mike*, a comedy about a professional sportswoman and her manager, written for her and Spencer Tracy. She impressed people at this time as being both brash and self-assured, but one family friend believed her to be 'shy, not in the ordinary sense, but with a profound basic shyness that was hidden under an arrogant front.' After she was taken out of school she relied mainly on her family for her close relationships, as she was to continue to do throughout her life, and grew progressively less easy with her peers.

By the summer of 1924 Kathy was planning to become a surgeon like her father and cramming for the Bryn Mawr entrance exams. She just scraped the required grades but after four years of private tuition was wholly unprepared for the scholastic and social rigors of college life. She swiftly became known as an eccentric, a reputation she did nothing to diminish with her habit of showering at four in the morning (she later said this was because she was too frightened to do so at a more social hour) and her extraordinary clothes. Having run so free as a child, she was accustomed to dressing for comfort rather than convention, which did not chime well with the habits of the day. As soon as she became aware of disapproval, she played up to it by dressing more and more outlandishly. More seriously, her grades were not good enough to qualify her for a medical major and she transferred to history. At some point in her sophomore year, however, Kathy decided that she was going to become an actress. In order to be eligible for college dramatics she had to improve her academic performance – and her grades took a dramatic upswing. As she said many years later: 'I discovered that although I wasn't brilliant, I could do it – if I worked. You can do anything, anything in the world, if you try hard enough.'

In her junior year Kathy took the lead in two plays, though with no particular success, and finally started to make friends. The breakthrough came in her final year with Bryn Mawr's traditional May Day celebrations, which took the form of an Elizabethan pageant. Kathy won the part of Pandora in John Lyly's three-act pastoral *The Woman in the Moon*, first performed for Elizabeth I in

Above: A wonderfully glamorous portrait of Kate taken in the late 1930s, at the time of her Broadway hit in *The Philadelphia Story*, and yet the strong-featured fourteen-year-old is still unmistakably there.

Left: Merion Hall, Bryn Mawr College. Kate arrived in Bryn Mawr in 1924 and at first found female college life a shock, but by the following year she was well established with a supportive group of friends.

Above: Kate in 1934, after returning from a European holiday by transatlantic liner even more freckled than usual. By then, however, she had landed her first Oscar for *Morning Glory* and her freckles had suddenly become charming.

1597. Instead of playing Pandora as a wispy, fragile creature, Kathy based her on her mother and gave a passionate, militant performance that eclipsed her fellow actors and astonished the audience. In that audience was a friend of the young theatrical producer Edwin H Knopf, who was preparing a season of summer stock in Baltimore; Kathy was given a letter of introduction to him and instantly took off for Baltimore.

Bursting into Knopf's office without an appointment, she handed the startled Knopf her introductory letter. He was less than impressed: 'Her forehead was wet, her nose shone,' he later recalled. 'She was tremendously sincere but awkward, green, freaky-looking. I wanted no part of her.' She firmly returned the day after graduation and haunted rehearsals for three days, until Knopf gave in and cast her in the walk-on role of a lady-in-waiting. This precipitated the first real row with her beloved father. While Kit was prepared to take the view that any career was better than dwindling into a wife, Dr Hepburn regarded acting as frivolous, pointless, self-indulgent, and altogether an unsuitable occupation for his strong-minded daughter. He was finally persuaded to give her $50 to cover her first two weeks' living expenses in Baltimore,

but it was many years before he became finally reconciled to Kathy's choice of career.

The Knopf company were amazed at the transformation achieved in Kate, as they called her and as she remained ever after, by lighting and costume. Knopf's leading lady Mary Boland, whom Kate studied incessantly and to the point of rudeness, said that when costumed and properly lit she suddenly lost her ungainliness and 'seemed borne up by light.' Her high-pitched nasal voice with its unmistakable Bryn Mawr accent, however, was a distinct drawback. One of her colleagues gave her a letter of introduction to Frances Robinson-Duff, one of New York's finest voice coaches, and in fall 1928, again grudgingly funded by her father, Kate moved to New York. Almost at once, and well before she was ready, Knopf offered her a last-minute lead in the out-of-town try-out of a new play *The Big Pond.* This was a disaster. Paralyzed with nerves, Kate played the role faster and faster until her lines became incomprehensible, and was fired the next day – an experience to be repeated several times before the lessons with Miss Robinson-Duff and her own determination began to pay off and she learned to pace herself. She had the immense advantage of a family sufficiently supportive (despite paternal grumbles) that she could afford to ride out the lean times, and this remained true throughout her early career; if she did not like a script she could turn it down. She was never wholly dependent on the film world for her survival.

Just the same, by December 1928 the Hepburn nerve was crumbling. She was hired to understudy comedienne Hope Williams in the Philip Barry play *Holiday,* a prophetic choice as she was later to film it to much acclaim, but the star was in rude health. Two weeks after opening night, Kate handed in her notice and, to the surprise of everyone including possibly herself, married Ludlow Ogden Smith, a charming, wealthy sophisticate whom she had met while at Bryn Mawr. He was by no means the first of her 'beaux', as she and her family termed them. Robert McKnight, later a noted sculptor, had been charmed but turned down, and it was a brave admirer who survived his introduction to the Hepburn menage, with its robust attitudes and wild arguments. Hepburn said later that 'I wasn't fit to be married. He was a nice man and no nice man should marry an actress.' After a honeymoon in Bermuda the couple set up home on East 39th Street in Manhattan; within two months Kate was dying of boredom and got herself rehired as Hope Williams' understudy. Effectively this was the end of the marriage, although Luddy remained a sympathetic and supportive friend even after his own remarriage. Even in her early and admittedly difficult days, Hepburn seems to have inspired an intense loyalty in her small, close circle of friends.

She spent the summer of 1930 with another close friend who had been a fellow-pupil of Miss Robinson-Duff's, Laura Harding, in summer stock in Stockbridge, Massachusetts, arguing ferociously with other members of the company but playing a wide range of roles and acquiring basic stage techniques which were to stand her in good stead. Fall 1931 saw yet another dismissal, this time from a new Philip Barry comedy in which she was to play opposite the English stage actor Leslie Howard. Howard could not bear her arrogance and mannerisms, and got her replaced after a week. Briefly but seriously, Kate considered abandoning the stage altogether.

It was the part of Antiope in *The Warrior's Husband,* a version of Theseus' wooing of an Amazon, which kept Kate in the acting profession and led her to Hollywood. The role of the militant Antiope was tailor-made for Hepburn and she wowed the critics. 'A tougher and more dynamic Peter Pan,' said the *Herald Tribune,* while for the *World Telegram,* 'It's been many a night since so glowing a performance has brightened the Broadway scene.' Although *The Warrior's Husband* only ran for 80 performances, in the course of it Kate acquired an agent, Leland Hayward, and a screen test with RKO. She was not at this stage particularly interested in Hollywood, having no desire to leave New York or the legitimate theater just as both were beginning to respond to her, and had to be persuaded by Hayward to do the test. She agreed on condition that she could choose the scene and her co-actor, thus

Above: In *The Warrior's Husband,* the play that brought Kate to the attention of Hollywood. The part of Antiope was originally intended for Hope Williams, whom Kate had understudied in *Holiday,* but it was a natural for the athletic Hepburn. Her first entrance involved descending a steep flight of steps with a stag over her shoulder to present it to Hippolyta, Queen of the Amazons. She hurdled the stairs three at a time, threw the stag down, landed on one knee – and the first-night audience burst into applause.

Left: The casually dressed image – canvas shoes and jeans – that at first infuriated Hollywood, although by the time this carefully posed portrait was taken the image had been harnessed to the studio bandwagon.

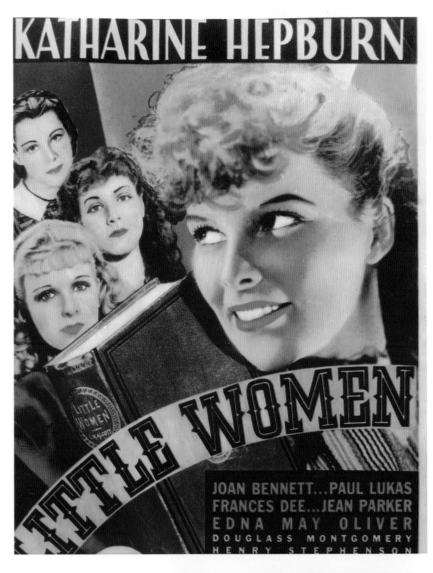

KATHARINE HEPBURN

LITTLE WOMEN

JOAN BENNETT...PAUL LUKAS
FRANCES DEE...JEAN PARKER
EDNA MAY OLIVER
DOUGLASS MONTGOMERY
HENRY STEPHENSON

Above: Publicity poster for *Little Women* (1933), one of Hepburn's own favorite movies.

Right: Kate with David Manners as the fiancé she sends away in order to care for her mentally tortured father, in her first film, *A Bill of Divorcement* (1932). According to *The New York Herald Tribune*, she 'is both beautiful and distinguished as the daughter, and seems definitely established for an important cinema career.'

establishing from the very beginning of her initially tempestuous relationship with Hollywood her determination that she should call the shots. She chose a scene from *Holiday*, already her favorite play, ensuring that she was at ease with her material, unlike most screen tests.

RKO at the time were casting *A Bill of Divorcement*, a Clemence Dane play about the daughter who abandons her own happiness in order to care for her once-great but now unbalanced composer father. John Barrymore had already been cast as the father and the young and promising George Cukor hired to direct, but David O Selznick at RKO was not convinced by any of the frontrunners for the role of Sydney Fairfield, who included Norma Shearer, Irene Dunne and Anita Louise. Hepburn's screen test decided him; as Cukor recalled, it was 'quite unlike any test I had ever seen before. Though she'd never made a movie, she seemed to have this very definite knowledge and feeling right from the start.' Still unsure about Hollywood, Kate made Hayward demand $1500 a week, an amazing sum for a newcomer and, even more amazingly, RKO agreed.

When Kate arrived in Los Angeles on July 1st, 1932, with Laura Harding for moral support, Cukor and Selznick were initially appalled at their rashness. As usual she was recklessly dressed, brusque and apparently self-confident in manner, although undeniably distinctive. She behaved like a star before she be-

Left: Publicity poster for *Break of Hearts* (1935). Kate and Charles Boyer were both praised for their respective roles as aspiring but unknown composer and eminent conductor but the film was not a success. They fall in love and marry; she leaves him when he deceives her with another woman, but returns with noble self-sacrifice when alcoholism threatens his career. The 'cheap emotionalism and shallow psychology' of the script was panned by the critics.

Below: Movie star Hepburn on the cover of *Screenland* magazine.

came one; on her first day she arrived for work in a huge chauffeur-driven hired car, dressed in a much-too-large sweater pinned together at the back and a pair of baggy pants. She and Cukor had an almost immediate confrontation over her wardrobe but Cukor stood firm and in the end it was Kate who backed down. She developed an intense respect for his judgment as a director and they also became close and lasting friends; Tracy rented a cottage on Cukor's estate for the duration of his liaison with Hepburn, and Hepburn and Cukor continued to work together sporadically for nearly 50 years. From the beginning she had a way with the movie camera, and Cukor knew how to use it. Her very first appearance in *A Bill of Divorcement,* a long tracking shot in which she silently descends a staircase, made it clear that Cukor was introducing a new star. And after some initial upsets with Barrymore, who made his inevitable pass and was equally inevitably rebuffed, Kate established a warm and educational relationship with her co-star, saying later that 'He taught me all that he could pour into one greenhorn in that short time.' The critics thought well both of the film and of Hepburn, and RKO heaved a corporate sigh of relief.

Kate's contract with RKO gave the company the option of keeping her, which Selznick now exercised, but it also guaranteed Kate her freedom for seven months of the year, when she inevitably gravitated eastward, back to family, friends and Fenwick. She never felt at home in Hollywood and never bought a house there. Her next film, *Christopher Strong,*

The Smart Screen Magazine
SCREENLAND
May
15c
20c in Canada
Katharine Hepburn
NEW CONTEST!
Gifts from
MARION DAVIES, CLARK GABLE, HELEN HAYES, MYRNA LOY, JEAN PARKER, MADGE EVANS—See Page 20

Above: Kate as the career-minded aviatrix who falls in love with a married man in *Christopher Strong* (1933), her second film.

was generally reckoned a bitter disappointment after the success of *A Bill of Divorcement.* It cast Kate as a flying ace who has a passionate affair with a married man, becomes pregnant by him but keeps the pregnancy a secret, and ultimately kills herself by pulling off her oxygen mask while breaking the world altitude record. Already, in her first starring role, she had established herself as the independent free-thinking woman she was to continue to play with variations throughout her life. For modern audiences this is part of her appeal but it was an image that fitted less easily into the 1930s. *Christopher Strong* was also interesting for its pairing of feminist star with feminist director, Dorothy Arzner, but unfortunately the relationship was less than successful. Kate was not the first choice for the film and Arzner resented the change, made just as shooting was about to start. And Kate reacted badly to

Arzner's demanding and autocratic way of working.

After one hit and one flop in her first six months, Kate went on to score a resounding success with her next RKO movie, *Morning Glory*, which won her her first Oscar. A wonderfully cliché-ridden piece which hardly bears watching today, this was loosely based on the story of Tallulah Bankhead, the classic tale of the smalltown girl who walks on to the stage an unknown and comes back a star – *42nd Street* without the songs. The screenplay was generally considered artificial, and Adolphe Menjou as the producer and Douglas Fairbanks Jr as a lovelorn playwright are neither of them at their best, but there was no doubt about Kate. The London *Times* reported that 'in a depressingly second-rate story she admirably mingles intellectual austerity with physical gaucherie,' while *Time* magazine acknowledged that:

From this immemorial fairy tale the delicate, muscled face of Heroine Hepburn shines out like a face on a coin. Of the brash little provincial she makes a strangely distinguished character, a little mad from hunger and dreams, absurdly audacious and trusting. Since *Christoper Strong* she has toned down her strident voice, taken off some of her angular swank in gesture and strut, found other ways to register emotion than by dilating her nostrils.

A reception like this guaranteed an Oscar nomination and the competition was none too strong. Although *Morning Glory* earned no other awards, it did get Kate the first of her four

Oscars without too much difficulty. Ironic that this was for one of her least characteristic parts as the girl from nowhere.

Above: A boyish Hepburn in her dressing room, with hair cut short for *Christopher Strong*. Clearly she had been earmarked for 'strong drama'; although some critics praised the movie, audiences were disappointed after the more immediate appeal of *A Bill of Divorcement*.

Left: Kate in *Morning Glory* (1933) as the earnest, idealistic and determined Eva Lovelace, the New England girl who arrives in New York to conquer the stage. After anguish and disappointment, and a sensation at a Broadway party when she gets drunk on champagne and recites Hamlet's soliloquy, she makes it to the top. As did Kate: the role won her her first Oscar.

Chapter 2
BOX OFFICE POISON
1933-1939

HEPBURN'S surprise success in *Morning Glory* brought her not only a sudden multitude of fans but also the first of a growing band of detractors, of whom Frank Nugent in *The New York Times* was one of the most virulent. He complained that her performances gave him the jitters:

The way she walks – those little scurrying steps, with her body inclined forward like a student roller-coaster who hopes desperately to reach a catch-hold before falling on his face. The way she talks – the breathless, broad A'd style, with meaningless breaks and catches, the so-soulfully brave, husky

tones with the pipe of hysteria beneath them. The way she plucks at this and that, and drapes her throat with tulle, and flutters and is so fearfully feminine that almost any normal woman would seem a Tarzan in comparison.

It is certainly true that the distinctly uncharacteristic part of Eve Lovelace did set the mold for a mannered Hepburn who was to reappear again in her later films of the 1930s. Perhaps she felt that if that was what earned her an Oscar, that was what audiences wanted. It was something of a reversion to her earlier semi-hysterical stage performances.

But then Kate at this time continued to be something of an enigma even to her close friends. Her determination to be a star had taken her to the top, but she was totally unco-operative with the Hollywood star system. Only Garbo had managed to retain her privacy and deny the fan magazines the intimacy that was expected between star and fans. Hepburn's icy treatment of inane press questions soon earned her the reputation of being spoilt and superior, and she was dubbed 'Katharine of Arrogance'. When the press found out that she was married, she first denied it altogether, then at a press conference responded to the question of whether she was still married with a stiff 'I can't remember'; asked whether she had any children, she replied 'Two white and three colored.' Hollywood couldn't cope with this mixture of reticence and levity and punished her accordingly. As one gossip columnist of the time indignantly put it:

A skinny, freckled, snooty typhoon Kate has hit Hollywood; she immediately set out to break all the rules and was as unpleasant and unco-operative as

Right: The face that glowers from this movie magazine seems to challenge anyone to dare dismiss her as a movie bubble.

Opposite: This studio shot shows Kate in the casual clothes that she preferred but which offended the conservative ranks of Hollywood, who expected women to conform to stereotypes.

The Smart Screen Magazine
SCREENLAND
September
15c NOW
20¢ in Canada

Katharine Hepburn

Is Katharine Hepburn a Movie Bubble?
Beth Brown Tells Her Hollywood Experiences
"I'm Afraid to Play with Garbo!" Says Leslie Howard

possible. She fought senselessly with practically everyone from top producers to lowest technicians. She was insulting and abusive to the press and gave out ridiculous and inane interviews in which she deliberately distorted the facts of her private life. She allowed herself to be photographed without make-up, in all her freckles, and even worse she dressed hideously in mannish garb – sloppy slacks, sweaters and men's trousers and suits. She hired a Rolls Royce to take her to the studio and she read her fan mail sitting on the curb outside the RKO lot.

None of this seems very heinous today, and much of it was Hepburn simply being herself, always an important part of her charm and success. Some of it was also due to the pressure under which films were made; most of Kate's early pictures were made in four weeks, *Morning Glory* in a staggering 18 days, which ruled out doing much other than getting up in front of the cameras and acting. Some of the legendary bad behavior was due to the terror she felt at first in going before the cameras; it was only with *Morning Glory* that she began to feel at ease with the camera and recognized how it enhanced her striking, unconventional looks. But there was also a real ambivalence in Hepburn at this stage in her career that Hollywood recognized and resented – stars were not supposed to be half-hearted in their allegiance to the system which had made them. On the one hand she demanded privacy, on the other she behaved in a way guaranteed to draw attention, with her mannish clothes and unorthodox escapades with Laura Harding. It was as if coming west was in some way equivalent to being let out of school and she was celebrating an adolescence that had been pre-empted by Tom's death. And the vaunted independence did not extend to financial matters. Soon after arriving in Hollywood, Kate confessed to her father that she had already spent her salary. Dr Hepburn was furious and insisted that she send him her checks and he would send her an adequate allowance, an arrangement that continued until his death. Her family remained intensely important and she returned east whenever she could to spend recuperative time at Fenwick. Years later she recalled her early days:

I became a star before I knew how to be a star, and then I thought, well, maybe I'd better learn how to do it. The first thing to learn is that nobody must ever know how terrified you are.

As the marriage with Luddy foundered, Kate found herself drawn into a closer relationship with her agent Leland Hayward, who was to remain the most influential man in her life, other than her father, until the advent of Spencer Tracy. Hayward was an unusually urbane and cultivated figure for Hollywood, scion of a well-established Nebraska family who had attended Princeton. He had married

Opposite: A haunted and vulnerable looking Hepburn with Doug Fairbanks Jr, her co-star in *Morning Glory*.

Left: A much retouched photo of Kate with Leland Hayward (sometimes wrongly identified as Luddy). In her autobiography, she writes: 'Life with Leland had no problems. . . There were solutions to everything. Joy was the constant mood. . . we had such fun.'

Below: In April 1934 the marriage to Luddy finally ended; in this delightfully casual shot, Kate is seen with Laura Harding visiting the ruins of Uxmal on the Yucatan peninsula, Mexico, where she obtained a divorce.

Right: Kate as the tomboy Jo March scandalizes her gentler sister Beth (Jean Parker) by climbing down the trellis from her first-floor window in this scene from *Little Women* (1933).

Below: 'As an antidote to the febrile dramas of the underworld and backstage musical spectacles, *Little Women* comes as a reminder that emotions and vitality and truth can be evoked from lavender and lace as well as from machine guns and precision dances.' – *New York Post*

Left: Hepburn and George Cukor lunching together in the studio canteen during the shooting of *Little Women*. He was her favorite director, from *A Bill of Divorcement* through to the last film they made together, *The Corn is Green*, 37 years later. She described him as 'primarily an actor's director. . . interested in making the actor shine.'

Texan heiress Lola Gibbs, divorced and then remarried her before he met Kate, and included some of Hollywood's most glamorous ladies, notably Ginger Rogers, Miriam Hopkins and, later, Margaret Sullavan among his clients. He was given to strolling through the executive offices of the movie world in white flannels and yachting sneakers, and requesting, and getting, outrageous salaries for his clients. He both liked and respected strong, clever women, and it was he more than anyone who helped Kate to overcome her nervy, self-defensive reaction to Hollywood hype, and to develop her own distinctive style both on and off screen. Hayward was not the only man to yearn after Kate, however; Doug Fairbanks, Jr, with whom she starred in *Morning Glory*, spent three months trying to persuade her to have dinner with him, only to have her plead a headache halfway through.

It was Hayward who, after the success of *Morning Glory*, managed to get Kate back with two film-makers who really understood her, Selznick and Cukor. They were in the process of scripting a screen version of *Little Women*, Louisa M Alcott's classic story of four sisters growing up during the Civil War. Cukor felt that 'like Garbo and *Camille*, (Kate) was born to play Jo. She's tender and funny, fiercely loyal, and plays the fool when she feels like it. There's a purity about her. Kate and Jo are the same girl . . .' Which of course was largely true; Kate's upbringing had been filled with just the same 'admirable New England sternness', and she threw herself into filming with a fervor that

cemented her already successful partnership with Cukor. Not that they didn't row, and once he even hit her after she had ruined an essential costume by spilling icecream down it, but their mutual respect survived and was strengthened by these exchanges. For the first time, too, Kate established a good relationship with the film crew and was delighted when, after a particularly outrageous bit of overacting on her part, a large ham was solemnly lowered

Below: With clergyman Gavin (John Beal) in her role as aristocrat dressed as gypsy in *The Little Minister* (1934).

from a crane and dangled before her. Cukor himself said that Kate cast 'a spell of magic, a kind of power that dominated even those scenes she's not in.' It is the first of Kate's films still to seem watchable today and her own favorite early movie, with its loose, episodic script very true to the novel, unfussy period detail and excellent playing by all concerned. According to *Time* magazine:

That *Little Women* attains so perfectly, without seeming either affected or superior, the courtesy and rueful wisdom of its original is due to expert adaptation by Sarah Y Mason and Victor Heerman [who won the film's one Oscar], to Cukor's direction and to superb acting by Katharine Hepburn.

Her next project was much less successful; she was anxious to be released by RKO so that she could take up the offer of the lead in Broadway wonder-boy Jed Harris's latest project, *The Lake,* and agreed in return to make *Spitfire* in a month for $50,000. This was a backwoods melodrama about a young tomboy faith-healer who falls in love with a dam-building engineer, feels herself deceived by him, kidnaps and cures a sick baby, but is almost lynched by her neighbors. A curious choice to follow *Little Women* and panned by the critics. *The New Yorker* said mildly that Hepburn's

'artistry does not extend to the interpretation of the primitive or the uncouth.'

Unfortunately her return to the stage was even more disastrous. It was motivated by a number of factors, not least her hurt at Leland Hayward's increasing fondness for the young Margaret Sullavan, whom he had signed six months earlier. Hepburn's relationship with Laura Harding had cooled in the course of *Little Women;* she was working too hard and well to be bothered with schoolgirl pranks and Laura returned east. Her personal life was confused and unfocused, but Luddy remained loyal and supportive. On her return to New York they moved into a large house, in which Hepburn still lives today, and she began rehearsals for *The Lake.* This was a brooding story of a passive and guilt-ridden young society woman whose husband drowns on the morning of their wedding. Noel Coward had warned Harris that the play, which had been a hit in London, would not travel well; Americans liked their heroines to be rebels not wimps, and Kate proved wholly unable to exude the necessary pathos. Harris, known as an anti-actor director, was extremely hard on her, with the result that she became confused, self-doubting and argumentative. In her autobiography, she describes the experience as 'a slow walk to the

Opposite: A relaxed and smiling Hepburn, in costume for *Alice Adams* (1935) and awaiting her cue, watches other members of the cast go through their paces with director George Stevens (in glasses).

Below: In *The Little Minister* Kate plays the glamorous Lady Babbie, who disguises herself as a gypsy and regularly visits the poor weavers in the nearby city. When the minister of the kirk falls for her, his parishioners are set to expel him – until they discover the gypsy's true identity. *The New York Times* was only moderately enthusiastic: 'Although dear Babbie's elfin whimsies are likely to cause minor teeth-gnashing among unsympathetic moderns, Miss Hepburn plays the part with likeable sprightliness and charm.'

LM-78

Right: Sylvia Scarlett (1936) is in many ways one of the most interesting of Hepburn's early films. As the young conman to Cary Grant's stooge, she puts on a wonderful show as a starving French boy in London's Hyde Park, but draws the line at using a serving girl's affection for Grant to steal her mistress's jewels. The artist for whom she falls (Brian Aherne) is sufficiently attracted to her as a boy to invite her to sit for him, but calls her a freak of nature when he discovers her true identity. The ingenious Grant manages to engineer a happy ending for all.

gallows.' When *The Lake* opened on Broadway on the day after Christmas 1933, the only reputation that was made was that of critic Dorothy Parker, who urged her readers to go to the play to see Miss Hepburn 'run the gamut of emotion from A to B.' After 55 performances the show closed and Kate sailed on a European holiday; two months later, at the end of April 1934, she divorced Luddy.

RKO, fired by the success of *Little Women*, were anxious for Hepburn to do another costume part and offered her J M Barrie's saccharine tale *The Little Minister*, in which a Scots aristocrat disguises herself as a gypsy and falls for the local preacher. Kate was at first reluctant, until she heard that her rival Margaret Sullavan was also in the running, whereupon she went all out for the part. The indefatigable Hayward, now back on warmer terms with his unpredictable star, negotiated her a six-picture deal with RKO at $50,000 a movie, then an astronomical salary. The choice of *The Little Minister*, however, proved a real miscalculation by both Kate and RKO, who put an unprecedented $650,000 into the budget, convinced that the new puritanism of the Hays Code made schoolroom classics a safe bet. Audiences, however, much preferred the musical escapism of Astaire and Rogers to the worthy piety of a labored period romance, and the movie lost nearly $10,000.

Pandro S Berman, head of RKO production since Selznick's departure for MGM, concluded that 'Kate wasn't a movie star . . . in the

Above: Kate was just one of many actors, writers and musicians who lined up behind President Franklin D Roosevelt's New Deal. Here they meet over a fish chowder at the presidential cottage to arrange a national radio show in support of the New Deal.

Opposite: *Mary of Scotland* (1936), with Fredric March as Bothwell, was one of a series of costume melodramas which did Hepburn's career no good at all.

Left: Kate as the dreamy Alice Adams, determined to show her wealthier girl friends she can land a suitable man (Fred MacMurray). The dinner to which she invites him to meet her family is, of course, a disaster – but equally of course, all ends well. The critics acclaimed her performance as 'striking and sensitive'; 'her masterpiece to date'; and she was nominated for an Oscar.

Above: Shooting a scene from *Mary of Scotland*; director John Ford, who became a good friend, is standing left in glasses.

sense that Crawford and Shearer were actresses able to drag an audience in by their own efforts. She was a hit only in hit pictures; she couldn't save a flop. And she almost invariably chose the wrong vehicles.' A verdict that was to condition the whole of her Hollywood career. RKO's next choice was no better; costume dramas were clearly out, and instead they

cast her in a slushy and inept soap opera, *Break of Hearts*, in which a budding composer (Hepburn) abandons her promising career to save an eminent conductor (a part written for John Barrymore and finally taken by Charles Boyer) from his alcoholism.

Alice Adams, her next picture, boded little better. Based on a Booth Tarkington novel

M O-Pub-A37

a hit and won Kate her second Oscar nomination (the award went to Bette Davis for *Dangerous*). *Time* said grudgingly that:

Though Katharine Hepburn is possibly the least versatile of all Hollywood's leading stars, it is precisely this limitation which makes her ideal for *Alice*. The woebegone grimaces, the expressions half-childish and half-addleheaded, so startlingly misplaced in her portrayals of women of the world, are precisely those which make her portrayal of a girl she really understands her masterpiece to date.

This success guaranteed Kate freedom of choice with her next project, and she went rejoicing back to Cukor, always her favorite director. He had long wanted to film *Sylvia Scarlett*, a deliciously absurd novel by Compton Mackenzie in which the heroine disguises herself as a boy in her travels with her conman father and a cockney adventurer. Cukor believed that Kate's *garçonne* quality was perfect for the part – she later played both Shakespeare's leading cross-dressing roles in *As You Like It* and *Twelfth Night* – and Garbo had had a stunning success with *Queen Christina*, in which she also played several scenes in man's clothes, only three years before. *Sylvia Scarlett*

Below: There was much speculation about the Hepburn/Howard Hughes romance. She met him on the set of *Sylvia Scarlett* and the affair blossomed while she was on tour in *Jane Eyre*, but fizzled out after about three years. In her autobiography Hepburn writes: 'It seems to me now that we were too similar. . . We each had a wild desire to be famous. People who want to be famous are really loners.'

Exclusive! **COMPLETE GUIDE TO ANSWERS IN $250,000 MOVIE QUIZ**

Modern Screen

NOVEMBER **10** CENTS

THE LARGEST CIRCULATION OF ANY SCREEN MAGAZINE

WILL AMERICA'S HERO, HOWARD HUGHES, *Marry* KATHARINE HEPBURN?

Hedy Lamarr's **LIFE STORY!**

about a dreamy, small-town girl who pretends to be well-born and wealthy in order to catch a husband, this looked like a low-budget program-filler. Despite difficulties between director George Stevens and his wayward star, however, Kate's performance caught the pathos in this unlikely heroine and struck a nostalgic chord for her audiences. The film was

Right: With Lucille Ball and Ginger Rogers in *Stage Door* (1937). Hepburn plays a self-confident debutante who moves in with a houseful of impoverished, stage-struck girls and thoroughly antagonizes them with her meticulous diction and large wardrobe – particularly when she wins the lead in a new production. One reviewer wrote: 'Never has Miss Hepburn been more compelling, more spellbinding. In the powerful emotional climax. . . she plays a tremendously effective scene which ranks as one of the best things she has done on the screen.'

was much more thorough-going in its transvestism, however, and audiences were horrified. Cukor and Hepburn, convinced that they had a hit on their hands, commissioned a sensitive and challenging script from acclaimed novelist John Collier. This explored the doubts about her own sexuality aroused in a woman forced by circumstances to undertake a prolonged deception, particularly when the hero shows every sign of finding her more attractive as a boy. Cukor then lost his nerve at the prospect of his star in trousers throughout, and tacked on a beginning and end that made a mess of the plot. Now a minor

Right: With Cary Grant and a butterfly net – and, incidentally, a leopard – in *Bringing Up Baby* (1938).

Left: In *Bringing Up Baby* Kate plays yet another spoilt heiress, but this time for laughs. When her brother in South America sends her a leopard as a present, she naturally turns to shy paleontologist Cary Grant for assistance. The result is 'undoubtedly the craziest, wackiest and screwiest farce that was ever saved from becoming idiotic by the talent of a delightful actress' – *Brooklyn Daily Eagle.* Hepburn herself has written: 'Cary was so funny on this picture. . . his boiling energy was at its peak. We would laugh from morning to night.'

classic and collectors' piece, at the time the film was a spectacular failure, although Hepburn herself got some good reviews and Cary Grant, as the raffish cockney, established himself as a real actor and not simply a charm merchant. He and Kate were to make three solid successes together soon, but meanwhile RKO recognized that they had a real problem with their biggest star – they still had not found the right formula for her.

Kate wanted to return to the stage at this point, always her preferred refuge when Hollywood proved particularly unsatisfactory, to play Viola in *Twelfth Night* at the Hollywood Bowl for the famed Max Reinhardt. RKO was having none of this, however, and put her into three successive costume dramas which almost finished her career off altogether. The first was the 1933 Broadway hit *Mary of Scotland,* a solid historical work quite unsuited to Kate's talents as actress or John Ford's as director, although it earned respectable reviews and led to a brief liaison between Hepburn and Ford.

Next came *A Woman Rebels,* an attempt to repeat the success of *Little Women* by casting Kate as a crusading journalist struggling against Victorian convention and bearing an illegitimate child rather than take refuge in marriage. *Time* felt that the picture was 'saved from total mediocrity by [Kate's] well-modulated performance', not a judgment that did anything for her failing morale. Nonetheless

RKO were so determined that her appeal lay in costume drama that her next film was another J M Barrie play, *Quality Street.* This period piece, written in 1906, is the story of a spinster schoolteacher who revenges herself on her erstwhile admirer by masquerading as her non-existent niece and making him fall in love with her all over again. Intended to be escapist fare, it went down like a lead balloon with Depression audiences. Frank Nugent of *The New York Times,* never a Hepburn fan, wrote that:

Miss Hepburn's Phoebe needs a neurologist far more than a husband. Such flutterings and jitterings and twitchings, such hand-wringings and mouth-quiverings, such runnings about and eyebrow-raisings have not been seen on a screen in many a moon.

Coinciding with the news that Leland Hayward had finally married Margaret Sullavan, the failure of *Quality Street* precipitated another return to the stage for Kate. The Theater Guild, which had once briefly employed her for *A Month in the Country,* now approached her to lead in a Broadway production of *Jane Eyre* opposite Laurence Olivier. In the event Olivier was unavailable and the pre-Broadway run in fall 1936 showed that the play was in an unfinished state; although it made a highly profitable provincial tour, closing in Washington, Kate and the Theater Guild decided against a New York opening. Mean-

Right: *Holiday* (1938) again partnered Hepburn with Cary Grant, she trying to smooth the path for her sister and her sister's fiancé, he as the fiancé who revolts against the stuffed-shirt money-making tradition he is about to marry.

Below: Publicity still from *Holiday*. According to the *New York Daily Mirror*, 'It is a film to which Miss Hepburn is entirely suited. Surrounded by a splendid cast, placed in staggering settings and clothes, given bright dialogue which modernizes the Philip Barry play, Hepburn makes an acting carnival of *Holiday*.'

while there was a new interest in her private life in the form of reclusive millionaire Howard Hughes, whom she had first met on the set of *Sylvia Scarlett* the previous year. While *Jane Eyre* was playing in Chicago, rumors of a marriage became so strong that a large crowd waited for hours outside the County Clerk's office on January 21st, 1937, expecting Hughes to apply for a marriage license. In the end the affair fizzled out – or one version has it that Hepburn turned Hughes down – and she spent the summer at Fenwick considering her future. She was 29, had made 12 films for RKO, of which only the first four were really successful, and was now well down in the popularity stakes after four flops in a row.

In the end a reluctant return to Hollywood seemed the answer. RKO badly needed her star quality and had no other female lead of her caliber, and so offered her a generous four-film contract guaranteeing her $150,000 a film. They finally recognized that what was needed was a contemporary story, and preferably a comedy. When Kate was offered *Stage Door*, she saw at once that it was a surefire backstage drama in the same mold as the Oscar-winning *Morning Glory*. The difference was that RKO hedged their bets by adding a second leading lady, Ginger Rogers, till then known only for her partnership with Astaire, and giving Kate third billing after Rogers and Adolphe Menjou. Other members of the strong cast were Lucille Ball, Ann Miller and stage actress Constance Collier, who became a lifelong friend. The *New York Times* hailed 'the return of Miss Hepburn from farthingales and tippets.' Her director, Gregory La Cava, found her an exciting actress to work with:

To win her, to beat down that proud impervious hauteur, is a challenge only the most virile and dominant male could afford to take up. That's the sort of man who should play opposite her . . . she's never had a leading man like that. They've always let her be the master.

Left: Hepburn and Grant
are caught practicing a
balancing trick for the
acrobatic sequence in
Holiday; Grant had been an
acrobat before he became a
screen star, and the
indomitable Hepburn was
game for anything
gymnastic.

Prophetic words which neatly sum up Kate's predicament in Hollywood – it was to be another five years before they were fulfilled.

The re-establishment of her prestige and sense of comedy led Kate into a three-picture partnership with her old co-star Cary Grant. The first of these was Howard Hawks' classic comedy *Bringing Up Baby,* with Hepburn as a spoilt heiress with leopard in tow, who sets her heart on Cary Grant's absent-minded professor – and needless to say gets him. The earnestness she brought to the part was inspired by Hawks, who emphasized the concentrated seriousness needed to achieve true screen comedy, and it remains a distinguished and timeless delight for just that reason. But for contemporary audiences across the US it was too fast, too sophisticated, too brassy, and at the time it was a commercial failure, despite some excellent reviews.

This was bad news for RKO. Normally Hepburn's pictures could be expected to make up any American shortfall in foreign revenue because, like Dietrich, she had always been more acclaimed in Europe than at home. But with war looming things were different. This realization coincided with the publication of an Independent Theater Owners of America list of all those screen artists considered to be 'box office poison'. The list included many of the best and most famous actors of the day: Garbo, Dietrich, Astaire and Mae West, and at its head was Hepburn. The fact that the female stars all played strong, independent roles, and that the most popular 'women' were Shirley Temple and Deanna Durbin, says much about 1930s film tastes. It was certainly too much for RKO who, after loyal support for their star through some bad years, cast her in a low-budget program-filler in the expectation that she would buy herself out of her contract – which she did.

Undaunted, Kate took herself and a long-cherished project off to Cukor. The screen rights for the Philip Barry comedy *Holiday,* in which she had understudied and screentested, were with Columbia, a minor studio who were delighted to make a one-off prestige picture with Cary Grant as the man who gets engaged to a wealthy girl, only to fall in love with Hepburn, playing the younger sister, and realize that some things are more important than money. The script was light and funny, the personalities worked, the setting was sumptuous and a familiar one to Kate, and the result was a delight. Cary Grant said at the time: 'As an actress she's a joy to work with. She's the most completely honest woman I've ever met.' But the theme had less impact in 1938, when Frank Capra's *You Can't Take it With You* had already won an Oscar, than when first aired in 1929, and again the film was a relative commercial failure. Hepburn said later: 'My career seemed to have ended with *Holiday.* I couldn't get a job for peanuts.' What made this worse was that she had tried hard for the lead in *Gone With the Wind,* with Cukor's support, but was passed over for an English unknown, Vivien Leigh.

Chapter 3
'I MAY BE A LITTLE TOO TALL FOR YOU, MR TRACY'
1939-1951

THE summer of 1938 was a bleak one for Kate. With Cukor and Selznick, her normal power-base, busy on *Gone With the Wind*, with no studio interested in her, and apparently unbankable even in comedy, it seemed that her career in Hollywood was over.

As always she spent the summer extremely happily, swimming, playing golf and tennis, and flying with Howard Hughes. Even the destruction of the family holiday home in a hurricane in September did not seem to daunt her – the Hepburns at once fell to planning the new

Right: Shooting a golfing sequence for *Bringing Up Baby*, Kate takes advantage of every spare moment to practice her game. Here her cocker spaniel watches eagerly as she approaches the green, while director Howard Hawks strides past in the background. Golf had been a favorite game since Kate's childhood, and was also one of the interests she shared with Howard Hughes during their three-year romance; his house in California backed onto the Wilshire Country Club golf course, and the couple would jump the fence to play.

house, using children's building bricks. There was something totally unquenchable about the whole Hepburn family. When things went well they might seem difficult, demanding, arrogant, but in adversity they rose to the occasion like champions.

And some friends remained stalwart. In the course of fall 1938, Philip Barry visited Kate in Connecticut with two possible new plays. One of these was a comedy about a Philadelphia heiress and her three suitors. Kate at once saw that this could be the vehicle for a glorious Broadway comeback and became closely involved in the final rewrite, so that the character of Tracy Lord was very much her creation:

Although I'd had a run of failures, I didn't want to go crawling back to a Broadway audience looking for sympathy or affection . . . I just wanted the curtain to go up and find me on stage in a nice dull scene being rude as usual to my mother, so they could all see that I wasn't trying to creep back to popularity, but being just as horrible as ever . . .

The result was a play wholly tailored to Hepburn's particular talents. Her good relationship with the Theater Guild made them the obvious choice to stage it, but finance was more of a problem. In the end the backing came in quarters, one from the playwright, one from the Guild, one from Kate, and one from the still-attendant Howard Hughes. Kate also bought the screen rights from Barry and, instead of a guaranteed salary, took 10 percent of the gross profits from the New York run and 12.5 percent of profits on tour. Perhaps under Hughes' influence, Kate had turned entrepre-

Above: With Van Heflin as the cynical young journalist in the stage production of *The Philadelphia Story*; Kate has described it as 'immediately full of hit atmosphere.'

Left: In the smash-hit movie version of *The Philadelphia Story*. Tracy Lord surveys her wedding presents with less than enthusiastic assistance from her ex-husband (Cary Grant), while her sister (a delightful performance by Virginia Weidler) and mother (Margaret Nash) look on.

Opposite: Hepburn and Tracy together for the first time in *Woman of the Year* (1942). When the project was first put to him, Tracy is supposed to have said: 'How can I do a picture with a woman who has dirt under her fingernails and who is of ambiguous sexuality and always wears pants?' After seeing *The Philadelphia Story,* he changed his mind.

Below: Another wedding scene, this time from *The Philadelphia Story.* The stuffy fiancé has fled, the reporter has offered for his 'golden girl, full of warmth and laughter and delight', but it is ex-husband Cary Grant who mops up the bride.

neur; her confidence in Barry's play was more than amply rewarded, since she made over $500,000 from the stage and screen rights to *The Philadelphia Story.*

In March 1939, when the play opened on Broadway after a successful provincial tour, however, the conclusion was not obvious, and rewriting continued right up until the last minute. Kate, remembering her destruction by the critics after the opening of *The Lake,* was awash with nerves and quite ready to believe the whole venture a disaster. But the critics thought otherwise: the *New York Post* found it 'difficult to take one's eyes off her,' while the *New York Times* recognized that she acted the part 'like a woman who has at last found the joy she has always been seeking in the theater.'

Initially Hollywood still played cautious, even after a triumphant post-Broadway tour lasting another 254 performances and grossing a cool $750,000. Then Louis B Mayer at MGM took a gamble and offered Hepburn a deal that gave her script approval and control of director and leading man. She enlisted Cukor, who added the prologue showing Tracy throwing her first husband and his golf clubs out through their front door, and Cary Grant, who demanded and got a hundred thousand

dollars and top billing. With James Stewart playing the idealistic reporter who also falls for the inimitable Miss Lord, the film was a natural. Interestingly, though, the Oscars went to Stewart and to the scriptwriter, and not to Kate. The Best Actress award went to Ginger Rogers, in the much inferior *Kitty Foyle,* and there were some who felt that this was the revenge of the 'little people of Hollywood.'

In a sense *The Philadelphia Story,* although it re-established Hepburn right at the top of the Hollywood tree, was the end rather than the beginning of an era. It was the last time she worked with Cary Grant, and it was perhaps the last example of a particular form of screwball comedy, with larger-than-life characters and well-heeled settings, before the advent of World War II rendered the genre obsolete. Hepburn's next project for MGM was very much a new beginning.

Various possibilities were aired before a new friend, Garson Kanin, showed Kate his script about the off-beat romance between a female political journalist and a tough sportswriter. Again doing her own wheeling and dealing, Kate showed this first to Joe Manckiewicz, her producer on *The Philadelphia Story,* and then to

Right: With co-star Robert Shayne in the Theater Guild production of *Without Love* (1942). The stage version went through considerable teething troubles but scriptwriter Donald Ogden Stewart tightened it up significantly when MGM decided to film it with Tracy as the male lead. *The New Yorker*, in fine acerbic style, wrote of the film: 'The somewhat metallic and stylized quality of Miss Hepburn's acting is almost perfectly suited to a role that is largely a vehicle for fashionable humor, and Mr Tracy's homespun behavior seems just about right for a man who really prefers airplanes to dames.'

Louis B Mayer. She wanted $100,000 for the authors, $100,000 for herself, and cast and director control; it is a measure of the confidence she inspired that Mayer agreed without a murmur. Kate wanted as her leading man an actor she had never met but much admired, Spencer Tracy. He had spent ten years in stock, marrying his leading lady Louise Treadwell in 1923. His big break had come in 1930, when he won the lead role in the prison drama *The Last Mile* and then co-starred with Bogart in the film version. By 1935 he was a major star, but was also known as having a major drink problem and could miss hours or even days of shooting. Despite this he was immensely respected for his understated acting technique: 'Any actor who's ever played a scene with Spencer will tell you,' said Clark Gable (whom Tracy in turn called 'the King'), 'There's nothing like it. He mesmerizes you. Those eyes of his – and what goes on behind them. Nobody's better than when they act with him.'

Tracy accepted the part in what by now was called *Woman of the Year* but was less impressed with Hepburn's reputation than she with his. The story goes that when they met she said 'I'm afraid I am a little tall for you, Mr Tracy' – at five foot ten in her heels she was only an inch shorter than him. 'Don't worry, Miss Hepburn,' he replied. 'I'll soon cut you down to my size.' Which of course is just what their on-screen partnership was about, and it was a conscious decision on the part of Kate and her advisers that this should be so. It had become

clear that there was no film future for her as a loner – she needed a film partnership to further and develop her career. To modern audiences there is something unattractive, even disturbing, in the metamorphosis of the arrogant, independent Hepburn of the 1930s social comedies into a fighter prepared and needing to be tamed by a man. In *Woman of the Year* the unlikely couple marry but Tess Harding (Kate) sees no reason to change her lifestyle or shoulder any domestic burdens, and on the evening that she is named Woman of the Year her husband walks out. Initially the ending was left ambiguous, but in the course of shooting it was changed to leave Kate firmly in the kitchen, making a mess of the breakfast.

Here at last was a performance that conformed to a recognizable stereotype and critics welcomed it. According to *Time:* 'As a lady columnist she is just right; as a working reporter he is practically perfect. For once strident Katharine Hepburn is properly subdued.' It was also plain to all those on set that the two stars had simply and sincerely fallen in love in the course of shooting. Until then Kate had perhaps been too much involved in establishing and re-establishing herself in the movie world, too well supported by her family and small circle of close friends, to feel the need of a more than transitory relationship. In an interview recorded early in 1991 to mark the publication of her autobiography, she firmly states her view that women's position in the world is so much less advantageous than men's that 'it makes me want to choke most of the men I know.' But by the time she met Tracy she had come to terms with her own abilities, finally felt secure in her chosen career and, as she memorably says, 'was in a position to be adorable to someone else.' She also recognized at once that she could be deeply useful. Half-way through making *Woman of the Year* Tracy vanished. He was finally found by Kate in a bar, brought home, sobered up and covered for, and so began a thirty-year relationship; one that did not at all reflect their on-screen relationship. In the films it is Tracy who is the strong, quiet, dominant partner and Hepburn who in the end succumbs; off-screen it was she who provided the solidarity and continuity, he who sometimes rebeled or wavered. Although the film partnership with Tracy certainly gave Hepburn's career an essential fillip – and the private relationship clearly brought her immense joy for many years – it is arguable that it actually came to hold back her development as an actress. The next real stage in her career does not begin until the making of *The African Queen* in 1951.

In 1942, however, after a brief pause while Kate returned to the stage to tour in another Philip Barry comedy, *Without Love*, which proved unready for Broadway, MGM reunited their clearly successful team in *Keeper of the Flame*. Although directed by Cukor, this proved a waxwork affair, the uncovering of a great man's Fascist past, and was the last time that the 35-year-old Hepburn was to play a straight glamour role. It also showed Kate playing second fiddle to Tracy, in another clear reversal of their private lives. Her own tastes ran to much more challenging material, and she put all her considerable energy into trying to persuade MGM to do a screen version of Eugene O'Neill's play *Mourning Becomes Electra,* his classic reinterpretation of the *Oresteia* set in the aftermath of the Civil War. MGM found the project too sexually provocative, however, and Kate made an impressive on-the-record press protest at the meretricious standards this decision implied. Her screen role with Tracy might require her to be submissive but the real Kate was a mature and increasingly formidable woman.

Her next movie venture, while Tracy made *A Guy Named Joe* and *The Seventh Cross,* was a real oddity, *Dragon Seed,* based on a Pearl Buck novel about the Chinese peasants' long struggle against Japanese aggression. As soon as both she and Tracy were free, MGM cast them in the film version of *Without Love,* which

Below: Keeper of the Flame (1942) was the second film to feature Hepburn and Tracy as co-stars, in a strongly anti-Fascist but not wholly successful piece. It was directed by George Cukor, who tried to achieve the moody suspense technique of which Hitchcock was the acknowledged master.

1256-2

proved considerably more successful than the play. The light-hearted story of a marriage of convenience between a wealthy Washington socialite and a woman-hating scientist, it fitted the Hepburn/Tracy team like a glove. And very much a team they were. The gossip columnists occasionally hinted at Hepburn's romance with a 'well-known actor', but Tracy was never named. This was as much in deference to his wife Louise, a well-respected philanthropist, as to his and Kate's standing in the movie world. It was Spencer's Catholicism that ruled out any question of a divorce and remarriage, but this seems to have suited Kate very well. As she told an interviewer in a rare moment of frankness about her affair with Leland Hayward:

For the independent woman the marriage problem is very great. If she falls in love with a strong man she loses him because she has to concentrate too much on her job. If she falls in love with a weakling . . . she always falls out of love with him again.

In effect she and Tracy maintained two separate households for the duration of their relationship, Tracy in a guest house on director George Cukor's estate, Hepburn initially in a hilltop home that had once belonged to silent-screen star John Gilbert. In 1946 Tracy was ill with stomach problems and did no work for almost a year and Kate ran his home as well as her own.

The problem was that with Tracy out of action MGM did not know what to do with

Above: Tracy, as the journalist in *Keeper of the Flame*, suspects that Hepburn, in the role of the widow of a national hero, played some part in her husband's death.

Below: Hepburn with Robert Taylor in *Undercurrent* (1946). The charming, wealthy man she has married is starting to behave strangely, and there is a mysterious brother who is never mentioned (Robert Mitchum) – but which of them is the psychopath and murderer?

1371-

Opposite: Tracy and Hepburn in the screen version of *Without Love*.

Hepburn with Tracy in *Woman of the Year*, their first film together and also one of their best. They both realized at once that in the relationship between political commentator Tess Harding and sports journalist Sam Craig lay the perfect screen partnership. Hepburn later spelt this out: 'I think on film we came to represent the perfect American couple. Certainly the ideal American man is Spencer; sports-loving, a man's man. Strong looking, a big sort of head, boar neck; a man. And I think I represent a woman. I needle him, I irritate him, I try to get around him, yet if he put a big paw out he could squash me. I think this is the sort of romantic ideal picture of the male and female in the United States.'

Kate. She was once more operating outside convenient definitions. *Undercurrent*, a minor suspense thriller co-starring Robert Taylor as a charming, wealthy psychopath and Robert Mitchum as the brother who is ostensibly the villain, might have worked if directed by Hitchcock, but Vincente Minnelli could not master the genre. Kate, as the psycopath's wife, was elegant but miscast. Even the movies with Tracy did not always work. *The Sea of Grass*, made in 1945 but only released in 1947 because MGM were unhappy with it, was based on a thoughtful novel about the conflict between cattle baron and homesteader but it did not suit either Tracy or Hepburn, who were wholly unconvincing as a stiff-necked cattle tycoon and his unfaithful wife. *Time* described the film as 'epically dreary,' while *The New Yorker* lamented that 'In *The Sea of Grass* Mr Tracy is grim, purposeful and, I'm afraid, occasionally ludicrous, while Miss Hepburn is as pert as a sparrow.' *Song of Love*, a saccharine, badly written retelling of the Robert and Clara Schumann romance, served her no better, though she worked hard to look convincing at the keyboard and earned some personal plaudits for her role. A 'sympathetic, earnest performance,' thought the *Baltimore*

Sun, while awarding the production as a whole 'a muted musical raspberry in B minor.'

In the late 1940s, largely as a result of MGM's miscasting of her in a series of deeply undistinguished films, Kate's popularity fell to an all-time low. Her early stand against Parnell Thomas, a McCarthy forerunner, and the House of Representatives UnAmerican Activities Committee did not help. In May 1947 she made an impassioned speech at an anti-censorship rally in Los Angeles in support of writer Donald Ogden Stewart, an early target, who had scripted a number of Hepburn films and was an old friend. Among other things he was responsible for tidying up *Without Love* into a natural Hepburn/Tracy vehicle, and it was another script for them, *Keeper of the Flame*, with its strong anti-Fascist message, that led to his indictment and enforced exile in London. As a result when Frank Capra cast Spencer in *State of the Union*, the story of a presidential candidate who almost sacrifices his political principles in his quest for leadership until brought to his senses by his estranged wife, it was not Hepburn but Claudette Colbert who was given the wife's role. Fortunately Colbert backed out at the last minute, pleading ill health – although she was probably

Below: Hepburn and Tracy as the cattle baron and his wife in *The Sea of Grass* (1947). Disturbed by his obsession with preserving his grazing ranges from the incoming homesteaders, she leaves him and has an affair with his bitterest enemy, played by Melvyn Douglas. *The New Yorker* commented gloomily: 'I suppose the general confusion of the plot isn't any worse than usual.'

Left: Kate's hair is brushed before the next shot on the set of State of the Union, while she plays the piano, a skill she mastered for her role as brilliant pianist Clara Wieck, wife of Robert Schumann, in Song of Love.

alienated by the final script, in which Tracy's role was dominant – and Capra went cap in hand to Kate.

The result helped to fix the Hepburn/Tracy partnership firmly in the public eye and is one of the tougher and more durable of their movies. Some think it their best, although at the time the critics were underwhelmed. It is a biting drama in which Capra exposes the shenanigans behind American democratic processes with none of the soft-focus sentimentality of *Mr Smith Goes to Washington*. Angela Lansbury walked off with the laurels at the time; 'as the adderish lady publisher,' said *Time*, 'she sinks a fine fang.' Capra, after a reluctant beginning, was smitten by his leading lady, and was to say later:

There are women and there are women – and then there is Kate. There are actresses and actresses – then there is Hepburn. A rare professional-amateur, acting is her hobby, her living, her love. She is wedded to her vocation as a nun is to hers . . . no clock-watching, no humbug, no sham temperament. If Katharine Hepburn made up her mind to be a runner, she'd be the first woman to break the four-minute mile.

Kate and Spencer's next project followed almost immediately on from *State of the Union*, after a brief and not altogether successful visit to England for Spencer to make *Edward My Son*. The removal to another continent at least allowed the pair to be together but their stay with Laurence Olivier and Vivien Leigh, old friends of Kate's whose wedding she had

attended, was beset by English damp and Vivien's obvious illness. While away, Kate was in regular touch with Garson Kanin who, with his wife Ruth Gordon, was working on a Hepburn/Tracy natural, called *Adam's Rib*. Cukor, Tracy's director on *Edward My Son*,

Below: With Spencer, Van Johnson and Angela Lansbury in State of the Union (1948).

and Tracy himself were both keen, and shooting started immediately on their return.

Adam's Rib is a battle-of-the-sexes comedy about a couple, both lawyers, who find themselves respectively defending (Hepburn) and prosecuting (Tracy) a woman who has shot and injured her husband after tracking him through the streets of New York to the love-nest where he is two-timing her. The tensions of the trial and the women's rights issues it raises spill over into the marriage, and the Gordon/Kanin partnership provided the Hepburn/Tracy team with some aggressively true-to-life dialogue even if, as ever, the story ends with capitulation by Hepburn. The movie was shot on location in New York, which made a pleasant change from tired Hollywood sets and even tireder Hollywood extras, and had a rather dour theme song by Cole Porter to give it an air of raffish respectability. The result was a resounding success, which sent the sagging box-office ratings of both stars soaring again, and at the time was regarded as the best of all their joint ventures. Bosley Crowther in *The New York Times* saw Hepburn and Tracy as:

The stellar performers in this show, and their perfect compatibility in comic capers is delightful to see. A line thrown away, a lifted eyebrow, a smile or a sharp, resounding slap on a tender part of the anatomy is as natural as breathing to them.

Off screen the partnership did not run so smoothly. Tracy was not an easy man, unsociable at the best of times – as was Hepburn – and never more so than when he was engaged on one of his periodic drinking bouts. He be-

came hostile to Kate's support, which he saw as interference, and resentful of any suggestion that he should seek professional help. By the time he had made *Malaya,* his next film, they were virtually estranged. To add to Hepburn's difficulties, the House UnAmerican Activities Committee was set on cleaning up the film industry, and on June 8th, 1949, published a long list of film people who were condemned as 'Communist appeasers.' Kate's name appeared on this along with that of Pearl Buck (presumably for writing a book on China) and Maurice Chevalier (considered a died-in-the-wool reactionary in Europe).

It was a good moment for a change. Shooting *Adam's Rib* in New York had reminded Kate of the joys of Broadway, and she finally acquiesced in a long-planned Theater Guild project to put on Shakespeare's *As You Like It* with herself as Rosalind, the duke's daughter who is banished to the greenwood and disguises herself as a boy. Her initial reluctance was as much to do with the failure of her cross-dressing role in *Sylvia Scarlett* as with alarm at playing Shakespeare. Her old friend Constance Collier, a fine Shakespearean in her own right, agreed to coach Kate; Shakespeare required a far greater range and color of voice than had been needed for any of the modern roles Kate had played on stage, as well as the ability to speak the verse with meaning.

Kate at 43 was an elegant, supremely fit woman, in a mold that might be more recognizable today than in the more indolent 1940s. Her voice had deepened, perhaps not unconnected with her heavy smoking, so that

Right: Hepburn with Tracy in *Adam's Rib* (1949), in which both played lawyers. As *Newsweek* described the movie: 'Here again is the famous battle of the sexes, strictly without benefit of August Strindberg and waged in the home and courtroom shared by Adam Bonner (Tracy) and his wife Amanda (Hepburn). Although both are lawyers and given to calling each other Pinky in their kittenish moments, there is no confusing their respective pronouncements on a woman's right to take a few compulsive potshots at a philandering husband.'

Left: With William Prince playing Orlando in the 1950 Broadway production of *As You Like It*. Although the production was an immense hit with audiences, the critics were less happy with her portrayal of Rosalind as a shy and limpid girl. As *The New York Times* put it: 'She is not a helpless, bewitched, moon-struck maiden swooning through a magic forest. . . Miss Hepburn has too sharply defined a personality for such romantic make-believe. . . And is this a New England accent we hear twanging the strings of Shakespeare's lyre?'

Below: A relaxed and candid moment from *Adam's Rib.*

the harshness that had drawn critical comment had mellowed. She had learned a greater confidence in her own acting abilities from Tracy, who was always described as a natural, and her knowledge of both stage and film technique was vast. The pre-Broadway tour of *As You Like It* was an immense success, and the play ran for 180 performances on Broadway. The public was fascinated by the thought of a famous screenstar on stage, although the critics were slightly less enraptured: 'Miss Hepburn's legs are always poetry,' said one unkindly, 'But I cannot help feeling that she mistakes the Forest of Arden for the campus of Bryn Mawr.' It was Kate's decision to play Rosalind not as a managing young woman, as might perhaps have come more convincingly from someone with her reputation and manner, but as a shy and restrained girl. Broadway was followed by a midwest tour, but meanwhile Tracy was anxious for a reunion and promised to stop drinking. He was then kept busy by MGM on *Father of the Bride* and *Father's Little Dividend*, keeping him committed to California until well into 1951. Kate was desperate for a script that would return her to Hollywood to be with him, but she was no longer seen as eligible for parts requiring either youth or glamour and there was precious little in the way of interesting parts for middle-aged women – a fact that still holds true today. To make things worse, the growth of television was threatening the movie world, which had to shoot bigger and better, more real and more exotic, to compete with this dangerous sibling.

Chapter 4
FINDING THE RIGHT SCRIPT *1951-1967*

JUST when it seemed that Hepburn's career might be declining into cameo roles, she achieved, with *The African Queen,* the greatest dramatic success and the best reviews of her life. Although it was Bogart who walked away with a well-deserved Oscar, the film was a landmark for Hepburn, who finally made the long-awaited transition from battle-of-the-sexes comedies with Tracy, costume dramas and high society romps to recognition as a great dramatic actress.

Sam Spiegel was one of a new breed of independent producers who had learned that, with money tight and television competing for audiences, the only way to get a film financed was to present a complete package, with bankable stars and director, to the money people. He wanted to film C S Forester's novel *The African Queen,* the improbable love story of a missionary's spinster sister and a cockney engineer, who together sail the boat of the title down a supposedly unnavigable African river and sink a German gunboat during the First World War. He knew he wanted Kate for the part of Rose Sayer, and in order to entice her to read the book he told her that he had already signed John Huston to direct and Bogart to star as Charlie Allnut, the uncouth, gin-swilling engineer (who becomes Canadian in the film). Hepburn was at once attracted by the book, the prospect of working with Huston and Bogart, and above all the idea of shooting on location in East Africa. She readily agreed, and the crafty Spiegel then shot the same line to Huston and Bogart, ending with exactly the package he wanted.

Before she left for the Belgian Congo in spring 1951, Kate returned home to Hartford to recover from the rigors of her *As You Like It* tour in the loving, chaotic family home. On March 17th, she and her father came in from a brisk walk in time for tea, to find Kit Hepburn dead of a heart attack. This was a devastating blow, particularly as Kate had to be on her way to Africa only three weeks later. 'What you do,' she said later, 'is move along, get on with it and be tough. Not in the sense of being mean to others, but tough with yourself and making a deadly effort not to be defeated.'

Opposite: Kate as the missionary's prim sister Rose Sayer in John Huston's *The African Queen* (1951), on location in East Africa, with Humphrey Bogart as the riverboat pilot whose idea of a well-equipped food store is 2000 cigarettes and two cases of gin.

Below: During the epic river journey the two make together, they have to pass beneath the guns of a German fortress.

Above: Location shooting in Africa lasted two and a half months, and Hepburn and Bogart then spent another six weeks in England, filming either at Shepperton studios or at Worton Hall. The footage of shooting the rapids was filmed on a back lot at Shepperton, using special effects. In the film the first set of rapids the boat navigates is a test; Charlie Allnut is sure that Rose will lose her nerve about their journey, but instead she is ecstatic: 'I never dreamed a mere physical experience could be so stimulating.'

She certainly needed that philosophy on location for *The African Queen*. The film contains some magnificent scenic shots but the heat and humidity were insufferable and living quarters basic, with a shower consisting of a tin barrel with holes drilled in it. The first two days it rained incessantly, and then an army of mosquitos attacked and Hepburn was kept busy with her bag of remedies. She was also laid low by a bad dose of dysentery which Huston and Bogart, who refused to drink the local water and stuck to bourbon, managed to avoid. The urbane and sophisticated Bogart hated Africa and relations between him and the ebullient Huston became strained. Kate too had her turn-ups with the director, who told her four days into shooting that she was playing the part of the spinsterish Rose much too seriously. He suggested that she base her interpretation on Eleanor Roosevelt visiting the war wounded, always with a smile on her face and full of hope. As a result Hepburn and Bogart discovered that they were playing a comedy as well as a war drama. Huston recalled later that:

He and she were just very funny together, one calling forth an unexpected quality in the other, and

the combination of their two characterizations brought out the humor in situations which on the printed page hadn't seemed very funny. Suddenly it was the story of a prim spinster becoming captain of a ship.

It is also the classic story of two ordinary, weary, middle-aged people finding in each other the inspiration for heroism; when she tells him what a story they will have to tell their grandchildren, the viewer is in no doubt that this tough improbable pairing will indeed survive to found a dynasty. The critics too were in no doubt about the quality of what they saw. Henry Hart in *Films in Review* catches the essence of the film's impact in a splendid piece of critic's euphoria:

The duel between this woman, as played by Miss Hepburn, and the dirty amiable ne'er-do-well played by Mr Bogart, is a masterpiece of acting, directing and dialogue . . . They have descended the river in order to reach a lake whose far shore is British territory. They are at the end of their tether and she prays: 'Oh God, tomorrow, when we are dead, judge us not by our failures but by our love.' That is a very powerful line, and Miss Hepburn reads it flawlessly. After she has spoken it her strength, her pride and her will are all gone. The back that had once been so straight crumples and the head that had always been so high dodders and falls to the deck and is still. She has been indeed laid low. One accepts not only her end but the end of the film. But the camera lifts up from the deck of the dirty boat, up from the almost lifeless man and woman, up from the swamp reeds and the jungle grass, up from the tops of the tropical trees, and there, a few hundred yards away, is the lake. The effect is breathtaking. It is an instance of the perfect utilization of pure cinema.

If *The African Queen* marked the start of a new era in Hepburn's career, her next project, *Pat and Mike*, signaled the end of another, being her last sparring comedy with Tracy, this time set in the world of sport. It was also the last time the Kanins wrote for the Hepburn/Tracy team, and the last time that the pair together worked with Cukor, although they were each to work separately with him again and were also to make two more films together, one memorable and one plain bad. Kate returned from Africa in summer 1951 and filming with Cukor did not start until January 1952. In the meantime there were changes to assimilate. During her absence in Africa her 75-year-old father had married the nurse who had worked with him for many years, and although family ties remained strong they could never be as close as while Mrs Hepburn was alive. Tracy, on the other hand, visibly needed Kate's firm management. He had become almost reclusive without her, drinking sporadically and smoking a lot. She changed his habits, making him take the inevitable Hepburn cold showers and

daily swim. He welcomed the prospect of another movie with her and *Pat and Mike* was well received, gaining an Oscar nomination, but there is something slightly mechanical about it, as of a well-worn and slightly tedious routine. This completed Kate's commitment to MGM, so while Tracy stayed in Hollywood to make *The Plymouth Adventure*, she flew east to undertake a second major career challenge in two years.

Above: Arriving at London Airport from Africa. Lauren Bacall was with Bogart throughout.

This was in fulfilment of a promise made to Michael Benthall, producer of her Broadway success *As You Like It*, that she would star in the first major production of George Bernard Shaw's play *The Millionairess* in London. Written in the 1930s and possibly based on Lady Nancy Astor, the play is not Shaw at his best or wittiest. The leading part of Epifania, the rich, spoilt, violent woman of the title and a symbol of the irresistible and corrupting power of money, is the only one with any life, and when the play premiered in Malvern, England, with Edith Evans in the lead, its muted reception denied it a West End transfer. Kate had already considered the project twice before; this time she believed that an inspired performance would transform it into great theater. Although she was supported by a strong cast, *The Millionairess* was very much a one-woman show and the critical reaction was mixed. There was no doubt that, by sheer force of personality, Kate triumphed in a piece originally dismissed as overwhelmingly bad: *The Times* praised her 'rhythmic beauty'; the *Daily Express* called her a 'human hurricane'; the young Kenneth Tynan said 'Miss Hepburn is not versatile; she is simply unique . . . Epifania is written on one note, but it is Miss Hepburn's note and she makes it into a cadenza.' This comment also neatly sums up the continuing query about Hepburn's art; it was magnificent but was it acting? As Philip Hope-Wallace, doyen of theater critics, said in his *Guardian* review:

Above: Conditions on location were tough – nothing as convenient as a changing room. Bogart said of Hepburn: 'That woman is sensational. I'll tell you frankly, she used to irritate the bejeepers out of me with all that 'mahvellous' talk. But when I got to know her I found that she's one helluva dame. She was up to her – well, she was up to here in mud and water for weeks, but she's a real pro and a regular dame.'

Right: Under Rose's high-principled influence, the boozy Allnut gradually sobers up (she tips the gin overboard); he even begins to shave.

. . . Such is Miss Hepburn's strident domineering stage personality that all these defects are forced to seem to us virtues . . . Miss Hepburn is that rare thing, the number-one size personality, and everything she chooses to do is right if only because it works so triumphantly on the audience. We are not merely bounced into accepting, we are bulldozed into belief.

American critics were still more dubious when the show opened on Broadway in November 1952, but it still ran for ten weeks to packed houses. Kate and director Preston Sturges tried to get a film package together but Shaw did not appeal to Hollywood. She later described this experience as 'the greatest professional disappointment of my life': that with two hits the size of *The African Queen* and *Pat and Mike* behind her, she still could not persuade the studios to finance the project of her choice. It was almost a year before she found something she thought worthy of her energies. This was a screenplay called *Summertime,* adapted by novelist H E Bates and director David Lean from an Arthur Laurents play about a mousey American secretary who fulfils a lifetime's ambition by going to Venice, and there has a delicate, understated, heartwarming affair with a charming, married antique dealer. Hepburn's presence brought a touch of distinction to an otherwise well-meaning but undistinguished movie.

On her way home from the Venice location to Tracy in California, Kate stopped off in London and was tempted into an even more adventurous stage project. Michael Benthall and Kate's co-star in *The Millionairess,* Robert Helpmann, were planning to take the London Old Vic Theatre company on a major Shakespeare tour of Australia, and asked Kate to join them as leading lady. She agreed to a six-month tour across the length and breadth of Australia, playing Katherine in *The Taming of the Shrew,* Portia in *The Merchant of Venice* and Isabella in *Measure for Measure.* Aware of how important the tour was for the Old Vic finances, she went out of her way to be civil to the local press, answering all the usual questions with surprising equanimity and showing only a trace of her normally barbed manner when asked if she were temperamental: 'Not at all. Look how charming I am being; of course I may drop dead at any minute.' The reviews of the tour were on the whole unimpressive but audiences were ecstatic.

The return home was less successful. During Kate's prolonged absence on Broadway and in London and Australia, Tracy had not only had an affair with Grace Kelly, but also and more seriously taken to the bottle to the extent that MGM were forced to fire him from the set of *Tribute to a Bad Man.* Many thought that this marked the end of his movie career, although he was nominated for an Oscar for *Bad Day at Black Rock* in the same year. From then until his death, Kate became almost custodial in her care of him, cutting down her own smoking drastically to help him give it up, exercising

Left: The *African Queen* has got bogged down in one of the myriad streams into which the river breaks up as it approaches the lake. The indomitable pair tow the boat as far as they can, and are finally washed through by the rain, but still disasters strike. The boat sinks; each thinks the other is drowned; but both are picked up by the German gunboat they had hoped to destroy with their home-made torpedo. About to be executed as spies, they are married by the German captain – and then the submerged *African Queen* collides with and sinks the gunboat. The movie ends with Mr and Mrs Allnut swimming triumphantly for the British shore.

with him, and accompanying him to France in 1955 to make *The Mountain.* From then on Tracy was seriously ill, with a weak heart and a badly damaged liver, and he became Kate's first priority for the rest of his life. As she says robustly in her autobiography, 'I loved Spencer Tracy. He and his interests and his demands came first . . . He did not – he *could not* protect himself.'

During the next five or six years, she fitted any filming she did into Tracy's schedule. If he was well enough to work then so did she, taking the best project that presented itself at the time. One distinctly disastrous result was *The Iron Petticoat,* a lackluster remake of the Garbo classic *Ninotchka,* co-starring Bob Hope and Robert Helpmann. *The Rainmaker,* filmed while Tracy was making *The Old Man and the Sea,* was more successful, and earned Kate an Oscar nomination for her role as the woman convinced by Burt Lancaster's young conman not only that he can bring rain but that she can find love. *The Observer* commented:

Burt Lancaster has never played the mountebank more sweetly, and Miss Hepburn's performance as the plain, unwanted woman who finds that it is within her power to become both beautiful and desired, again compels admiration for her qualities as an actress and the choice architecture of her face.

The obvious answer to the limitations caring for Tracy placed on Hepburn's work schedule was another joint film. Unfortunately *Desk Set* was a thin comedy, with the usual warmed-up spinster role for Kate, but audiences welcomed the pair's return to the screen and, as Bosley Crowther of *The New York Times* said:

They lope through this trifling charade like a couple of oldtimers who enjoy reminiscing with simple routines. Mr Tracy is masculine and stubborn, Miss Hepburn is feminine and glib. The play is inconsequential.

The problem was to find anything worthwhile to do; long tours were out and Hollywood was having its usual difficulty in finding her suitable parts. The opportunity to play several roles in repertory in the short season at the American Shakespeare Festival, Stratford, Connecticut, was ideal. In summer 1957 Kate again played Portia in *The Merchant of Venice,* and added Beatrice in *Much Ado About Nothing*

Below: *Pat and Mike* (1952) was the last of the sparring comedies Kate made with Spencer. She played a college PE teacher who is signed as an all-round professional athlete by smooth, fast-talking sports promoter Mike Conovan (Tracy). She looked radiant and was in tremendous physical shape, swimming, biking, boxing and playing basketball in the film. Bosley Crowther of *The New York Times* was impressed that she 'can swing a golf club or tennis racquet as adroitly as she can sling an epigram.'

Left: As the American secretary who blooms in Venice in *Summertime* (1955). Kate later described David Lean as 'one of the most interesting directors I ever worked with.'

Below: Hepburn as the impossible Epifania in the stage production of George Bernard Shaw's *The Millionairess*, which premiered in London and moved to New York in 1952. Here she attacks the unfortunate Adrian Blenderbland (Cyril Ritchard) for calling her father a bore.

Right: In *The Rainmaker* (1956) Kate plays Lizzie, the clever, competent only daughter in a household of sons, convinced that no man is interested in her, despite the cackhanded machinations of her father and brothers to involve her with the deputy sheriff. Burt Lancaster's conman not only talks her father into believing he can bring rain – for a price – but also makes Lizzie accept that she is beautiful: 'There's no such thing as a plain woman.'

Below: Lizzie has prepared a feast and put on her best dress for the deputy sheriff, but her family fail to persuade him to come to supper. Instead conman Starbuck turns up, and by the end of the film Lizzie has both of them at her feet.

Left: *Desk Set* (1957) recycled Hepburn and Tracy yet again as the all-American couple. This time she is the library boss who feels her staff and livelihood threatened by the electronic brain invented by a methods engineer (Tracy).

Below: Kate with Spencer in the 1960s, when she more or less abandoned film-making to devote herself to him. She writes in her autobiography: 'Love has nothing to do with what you are expecting to get – only with what you are expecting to give – which is everything.'

to her repertoire, while in 1960, at the grand age of 53, she received some of her best stage reviews to date with her surprisingly sensual playing of Cleopatra in *Antony and Cleopatra*, although her Viola in *Twelfth Night* (24 years after her first breeches part in *Sylvia Scarlett*) was less successful.

Hepburn's only film performance in the three years that separated her two Shakespeare seasons was the screen version of *Suddenly Last Summer*, Tennessee Williams' 'everyday story of homosexuality, madness and cannibalism in the Deep South', as Sheridan Morley has memorably described it. An intensely gothic creation, this had a wonderful role for Kate as the devoted mother who tries to get her niece (Elizabeth Taylor) lobotomized by bribing a brilliant young neurological surgeon (Montgomery Clift), so that she cannot reveal the details of how her cousin, Hepburn's son, has been raped, murdered and eaten on a North African beach by the boys he was trying to seduce. In 1959 this was strong stuff and a brave choice by Hepburn, who had reached a stage in her career when she could not only afford but actively welcomed risk; the critics were alarmed but, on the whole, appreciative, and the film marked the first role in her final glorious phase as an actress of formidable dowagers.

It was 1961 before she again emerged from her seclusion with Tracy, this time tempted out by the chance of making a film of Eugene O'Neill's classic story of the self-destructive Tyrone family, *Long Day's Journey into Night*,

Left: In her first season with the American Shakespeare Festival at Stratford, Connecticut, in 1957, Kate played Beatrice, the acid-tongued heroine of *Much Ado About Nothing.* The critic of the *New York Herald Tribune* wrote that 'The lines Shakespeare gave Beatrice are eminently suited to Miss Hepburn and she reads them with a lean suggestion of hysteria that makes them scratch arrogantly at her Benedick, whom she feuds as a prelude to love.

15 years after she had failed to get MGM interested in *Mourning Becomes Electra.* The result, though heavy going for movie audiences at four hours' duration, is superbly played by an all-star cast, which includes the English stage and screen actor Ralph Richardson as the father and Jason Robards Jr and Dean Stockwell as the sons, as well as Hepburn as the tragic, drug-addicted mother. She herself has described the film as 'an inspiration to do'; the director, Sidney Lumet, shot it in sequence, extremely rare in movie-making, and the result was in many ways Hepburn's greatest professional achievement. The normally hyper-critical Pauline Kael concluded that 'from being perhaps America's most beautiful comedienne of the thirties and forties' Kate had 'become our greatest tragedienne.'

Kate's own life took a tragic turn at this time, however, first with Tracy's serious attack of emphysema and then with the death of her father on November 20th, 1962. Thereafter, for five years, she retired totally from public life to devote herself to the increasingly dependent Tracy. He continued, with her support, to make the occasional film, however, particularly if Stanley Kramer, with whom he had made his Oscar-winning *Judgment at Nuremberg* in 1961, was to be involved. It was Kramer who succeeded in persuading the Hepburn/Tracy team back on screen one more time in 1967, when Tracy was known to be mortally ill, to make the all-time weepie *Guess Who's Coming to Dinner,* about the liberal couple whose principles falter when their daughter

brings home a black fiancé. This was an immense act of faith on Kramer's part; Tracy was far too sick to be insurable, and Kramer and Hepburn had to agree to forfeit their salaries, in the event of Tracy's death before the film was finished, in order to persuade the studio, Columbia, to finance it. The result is a classic as much for its failures as for its successes. Supposedly a great liberal picture about race relations, it loads the dice so heavily in favor of the brilliant Rhodes scholar (Sidney Poitier), with his high-flying World Health Organization posting to Geneva, that some viewers wondered at the time whether even the daughter of Hepburn and Tracy could be worthy of him, though that did not seem to be the issue. But the acting is brilliant and the timing impeccable, particularly the moment when the young man's parents arrive and swing Tracy's father figure in favor of the match by their obvious disapproval. And Tracy's final speech, a plea for social tolerance and a declaration of his love for his wife, is intensely dramatic and painfully moving. The normally rebarbative *New Yorker* said:

When, at its climax, he turns to her and tells her what an old man remembers having loved, it is, for us who are permitted to overhear him, an experience that transcends the theatrical.

Ten days after shooting was finished, Hepburn arrived as usual one morning at the small house on George Cukor's estate that Tracy lived in, to find him slumped over a glass of milk at the kitchen table, dead of heart failure.

Opposite: Kate as the terrifying Mrs Venable in Tennessee Williams' *Suddenly Last Summer,* filmed in 1959. Her role was described as one that 'even in its evil has a perverted charm.'

Chapter 5
THE TRIUMPHANT
SURVIVOR *1967-*

Below: By the time this glowing portrait was taken, critics had taken to describing Kate as 'beautifully boned', 'a superb tragedienne.'

TRUE to the last to the discreet role she had played in Tracy's life, Hepburn, having called the doctor, Cukor and Tracy's brother Carroll, then retired from the scene and did not attend his funeral. Instead, with Phyllis Wyborn, the faithful secretary and companion she had inherited from her old friend Constance Collier, she returned to Fenwick and her family. Her sisters and brothers were now grandparents and the house was full of life, but for once this was not enough and she and Phyllis took a house on Martha's Vineyard for the summer of 1967. The public was swift to cast her in the role of widow manqué; only two days after Spencer's funeral the *Los Angeles Times* was referring to the liaison as 'an association as beautiful and dignified as any this town has ever known.' When awarded an Oscar for her role in *Guess Who's Coming to Dinner*, she accepted it on the basis that it was as much for Tracy as for herself, confiding to her then director, Bryan Forbes, that 'They don't often give it to old girls like me.'

More to the point for the bereaved Hepburn was the arrival toward the end of the summer of the script for *The Lion in Winter*, a stormy drama about the last meeting between Henry II of England, his estranged and imprisoned queen, Eleanor of Aquitaine, and their three sons, in an effort to settle the succession to the throne. Kate agreed instantly to play the ageing, anguished but still regal Eleanor, and Peter O'Toole was signed for the more youthful Henry. O'Toole was known as a tyrant on set but he was no match for the formidable Hepburn. 'Peter, stop towering over me,' she would order. 'Come and sit down and try to look respectable.' And meekly the normally unmalleable O'Toole would do so, maintaining that 'she has been sent by some dark fate to nag and torment me.' The relationship became one of affectionate warfare, adding immensely to the film's impact; O'Toole described his co-star, 24 years his senior, as 'a

PETER O'TOOLE   KATHARINE HEPBURN

cross metween Medusa and Tugboat Annie.' The result is a riot; pop history at its best, with the royal family spending its Christmas holiday scheming, quarrelling and backstabbing. The script is sharp and self-mocking, always hovering on the edge of vulgarity but never quite succumbing. 'It's 1183 and we're barbarians,' announces Hepburn smugly, and 'Hush, dear, mother's fighting,' and, after a long list of horrors including adultery, annulment, incest and disinheritance, 'What family doesn't have its little ups and downs?' It was a heaven-sent part and Kate fell on it with all the ferocious energy and commitment at her disposal. The critics were flattened and finally started to accord her the over-effusive tributes due to an iconic star. *The Times* saw the role as:

Arguably the performance of her career. Playing the relentlessly intelligent, ambitious, cunning, devious and yet after all, when one least expects it, human and vulnerable Eleanor of Aquitaine, she finds possibilities both in herself and in the text which we would hardly have guessed at.

The film gained seven Oscar nominations and three awards, including one for Kate, her third in total (making her the most honored Hollywood actress ever) and her second in a row, a staggering 35 years after the first for *Morning Glory*. In audiences' eyes she could now do no wrong. Hepburn herself was as detached about her deification as she had been about the 'box office poison' label in the 1930s: 'Now that I am Saint Katharine,' she said, 'it is fashionable

Above: Publicity poster for *The Lion in Winter* (1968), which earned Kate a third Oscar. She recalls in her autobiography that on one occasion during shooting the make-up man she shared with Peter O'Toole was working on O'Toole, despite the fact that Hepburn was filming first. She grabbed the make-up man, swatted O'Toole on the head, and retired triumphant – to be followed presently by O'Toole wrapped in bandages, on crutches, and moaning. 'You can see we had fun,' she concludes.

to say that I am a beauty with a well-proportioned face. But when I was beginning they thought I was just a freak with a lot of freckles.'

Regrettably her next release was a much less successful movie, both critically and commercially. *The Madwoman of Chaillot*, the film version of a classic play by Jean Giraudoux, is the story of an eccentric countess who plans to save Paris from a group of war-minded capitalists who want to turn it into a giant oilfield. The director should have been John Huston,

with whom Kate had worked on *The African Queen*, but he opted out two weeks before filming began and Bryan Forbes failed to rescue the resulting muddle, despite an amazingly starry cast.

Before she had left for Europe to work on these two costume dramas, Kate's old friend Irene Selznick had persuaded her to audition for the role of the ageless couturière Coco Chanel, in a musical written by Alan Jay Lerner (of *My Fair Lady* fame) and André Previn. At first Kate laughed uproariously at the

Above: With O'Toole as Henry II in one of their more amicable moments during *The Lion in Winter*. Their mutual respect and affection is no match for their political ambitions.

Opposite: Perfectionist to the last, Kate checks a camera angle on the set of *Guess Who's Coming to Dinner* (1967), her last film with Tracy.

thought of singing in public then, as ever, she rose to the challenge, took singing lessons, and landed the part. Chanel herself approved the choice, and Kate recognized a lot of herself in the 86-year-old Parisian:

We're two females who have never been intimidated by the world, who have never shifted our styles to conform to public opinion . . . her capacity for survival is what really fascinates me.

So, at the age of 62, she committed herself to the punishing Broadway schedule of eight performances a week.

The idea of casting Kate as Coco was a stroke of genius but the musical, with immensely complicated sets by Cecil Beaton, precious little plot and an undistinguished score by Previn, was a dinosaur of a piece at a time when the old-fashioned spectacular Broadway musical seemed an anomaly. Reviewers were unimpressed but, as *The New York Times* observed: 'The show has become a showcase, a form of endearment, a gesture of assent, an open palm of respect.' Regardless of reviews, Kate on Broadway proved capable of packing the theater every night for six months, an achievement she was to match twice more

in the next decade. After shunning publicity and adulation for nearly four decades, she had become a massively popular cult figure – and found that she liked it, that it helped to fill the gaping hole left by the deaths of her father and of Tracy, the two fundamental male influences in her life.

Her first movie of the early 1970s was less successful; it was the usual problem of finding the right script. The film version of Euripides' *The Trojan Women,* with Vanessa Redgrave, Irene Papas and Genevieve Bujold, failed to rise above the staginess of the screenplay and the very disparate accents of the four principals, but as Kate said: 'I've never done Greek tragedy and before my time runs out I'd like to have tried everything.' She also longed to make another film in Hollywood, and all seemed set fair for a film version of Graham Greene's *Travels with My Aunt* – until MGM decided that they did not like the version of the script with which Kate had become closely identified, and wanted to show the character as a younger woman in flashback. So once again, for the last time in her life, and immediately after winning two successive Oscars, Kate Hepburn was fired from a movie.

Above: With Nanette Newman in *The Madwoman of Chaillot* (1969), a tame follow-up to *The Lion in Winter.* The decision to update Giraudoux's timeless fantasy of a play displeased John Huston, the original director, and gave an earth-bound heaviness to what should have been a lightweight whimsy.

Opposite: Despite her continued vitality and glowing good looks, Kate became sensitive in her later years about the crepiness of her neck, and from the 1960s on was invariably shrouded up to the chin.

Above: Coco was something of an anachronism as a musical, but it played to packed houses. Here Coco (Hepburn) chronicles her early career for a young model (Gale Dixon) whom she has taken under her wing.

Right: Rooster Cogburn was an attempt to recapture some of the atmosphere of both *The African Queen* and John Wayne's Oscar-winning role in *True Grit*. One reviewer summed up the prevailing reaction when he wrote: 'The plot is negligible, the direction minimal, but the two Powerhouses carry it through entertainingly. Who could ask for more?'

Opposite: Hepburn in Wales in 1978 for the making of the television play *The Corn is Green.*

Instead, after *The Trojan Women*, she made a number of television films, a new medium for her but a quick and economical way of making a permanent record of a classic play. The first of these was Edward Albee's *A Delicate Balance* (1973), directed by Tony Richardson and co-starring Paul Scofield, to be followed by Tennessee Williams' *A Glass Menagerie.* In 1975 she returned to London to make *Love Among the Ruins*, a delightful Edwardian love story between a former Shakespearean actress and the famous barrister with whom she once had a forgotten affair; the barrister was played by her old friend Laurence Olivier, the first time they had acted together. Another old friend, George Cukor, directed, and it was with him that Kate again returned to the UK in 1979 to make *The Corn is Green,* Emlyn Williams's story of an English teacher in a Welsh mining village.

Her only major Hollywood movie of the 1970s, *Rooster Cogburn,* co-starred another craggy survivor, though in a rather different mold – John Wayne. The film was dismissed as a poor follow-up to *The African Queen* and *True Grit* and memorably panned by the *New Yorker* as 'just a belch from the Nixon era.' But

the two stars, despite their fundamentally different political viewpoints, developed a healthy respect for each other and a good rapport, and commercially the movie was a hit. Another Broadway venture, *A Matter of Gravity*, co-starring a pre-Superman Christopher Reeve, again brought the audiences streaming in, despite the slightness of the play, as did *West Side Waltz* in 1981. Hepburn had concluded that there was a lot more potential in being an old stage actress than an old screen actress.

She could, however, be lured back on screen by the right project. *Olly Olly Oxen Free* (1979), a delicious, absurd film about an eccentric junkyard proprietress who accidentally goes hot-air ballooning with two children she has befriended, was hampered by a leaden script but 'they let me play most of it up in a balloon and how often do you get to do that at 70?' In 1985 she made *The Ultimate Solution of Grace Quigley*, an extremely black comedy about an elderly woman's flourishing euthanasia business. But the late film for which she will always be best and most fondly remembered is, of course, *On Golden Pond*.

On Golden Pond, a play by Ernest Thompson, had had a reasonably successful run first off and then on Broadway in 1978. It is the story of a couple, married 50 years, who come to spend the summer in their cottage on Golden Pond in Maine. Norman has a heart condition and his wife Ethel, ten years his junior, is battling to keep him alive and happy – an uphill task given his disposition, and

Above: Two giants of the screen together at last in *On Golden Pond* (1981); both won Oscars for their roles, although Hepburn's was more a sentimental tribute to her career as a whole than an award for this particular part, which was anyway less substantial than Fonda's and which she unselfishly ensured did not compete.

Right: With Jane Fonda, who plays her father's daughter.

Opposite: Hepburn continues to live contentedly in the same New York brownstone that she bought soon after her marriage, surrounded by devoted friends and family.

Left: 'I'm a romantic painter of landscapes and people. I've always been more interested in what painters have to say – because painting interests me more than acting. You do it by yourself, you don't say somebody else's lines.'

further complicated by the arrival of their divorced daughter, determined to thrash out her relationship with her father before he dies, plus her appalling lover and his difficult 13-year-old son. A sentimental piece, this would probably never have made it on to film, had Jane Fonda not seen it as a vehicle for her dying father to make his public farewell. She acquired the screen rights and put up her own salary as insurance for her father, just as Hepburn had done for Tracy 14 years earlier. Given the background the part of Ethel was irresistible to Hepburn even though, as with her films with Tracy, the male lead was the key to the story. Extraordinarily she and Henry Fonda had never met. On the first day of shooting she gave him Tracy's favorite hat, and he wore it throughout the film.

The result is film history. The background to the movie was common knowledge and this, plus impeccable if tear-struck acting, lift a waffling, potentially forgettable play (described by one acerbic critic as a 'hunk of sub-Chekhovian New England marshmallow') into the realms of mythology. *On Golden Pond* articulated for 1980s audiences a growing disenchantment with the violent, high-tech movies which dominated the box offices, and a renewed desire for the old-fashioned values of warmth and humanity which Hollywood had once been so adept at expressing. Middle-aged filmgoers returned to the cinemas in droves and the film became the runaway hit of the season. *Newsweek*'s review reflected the almost unanimously favorable critical judgment:

The story is sentimental. But call it what you may – middlebrow, manipulative – the movie lives and breathes and has the power to pluck a responsive chord in all but the most cynical viewer . . . Hepburn is radiant and physically astonishing, whether swinging from the arms of a chair or diving from a boat . . . an intelligent tearjerker, a handcrafted heartbreaker.

It was Fonda who received the lion's share of the accolades at the time; some critics thought that Hepburn's performance was over-sentimentalized. She was also handicapped by an eye condition which made her look permanently weepy (a legacy of her famous fall into a polluted Venetian canal for *Summertime*) and the onset of Parkinson's disease, which gave her the shakes. Fonda's Academy Award was widely predicted but when Hepburn too carried off an Oscar, breaking her own record, it created a sensation.

In 1984 a survey of 4,500 American teenagers asked who they would name as their ten contemporary heroes. The only woman on the list, which included such names as Michael Jackson and Clint Eastwood, was Katharine Hepburn, at number seven one ahead of the Pope. She was 77 at the time. Once asked if she had ever planned to retire, she replied: 'In a lifetime of gardening, I have never yet seen a laurel on which one could rest really comfortably. There are no laurels in my life, just new challenges.'

Opposite: As the warm-hearted and inspiring teacher Miss Moffat in a television version of Emlyn Williams's play *The Corn is Green*, which also starred Anna Massey, Toyah Wilcox and Patricia Hayes, and was directed by one of Kate's oldest friends, George Cukor.

Left: In *The Ultimate Solution of Grace Quigley*, Hepburn addressed herself in her uncompromising way to old age, playing an elderly lady who hires a professional hit man (Nick Nolte) to put her out of her misery. Unfortunately the movie was not a success.

Below: Hepburn in the White House in December 1990, being applauded by fellow Kennedy Center honorees Billy Wilder (left) and Dizzy Gillespie.

Opposite: 'I have no idea how Spence felt about me. I can only say that I think if he hadn't liked me he wouldn't have hung around.'

Filmography

Below: *Bringing Up Baby* is one of Kate's happiest films of the 1930s and the first in which her skills as a comedienne are fully exploited, but it coincided with a downturn in her popularity.

1932
A Bill of Divorcement, DIR. George Cukor, co-starring John Barrymore, Billie Burke

1933
Christopher Strong, DIR. Dorothy Arzner, co-starring Colin Clive, Billie Burke
Morning Glory, DIR. Lowell Sherman, co-starring Douglas Fairbanks Jr, Adolphe Menjou, Mary Duncan, C Aubrey Smith

Little Women, DIR. George Cukor, co-starring Joan Bennett, Paul Lukas

1934
Spitfire, DIR. John Cromwell, co-starring Robert Young, Ralph Bellamy
The Little Minister, DIR. Richard Wallace, co-starring John Beal, Alan Hale

1935
Break of Hearts, DIR. Philip Moeller, co-starring Charles Boyer
Alice Adams, DIR. George Stevens, co-starring Fred MacMurray, Fred Stone

1936
Sylvia Scarlett, DIR. George Cukor, co-starring Cary Grant, Brian Aherne
Mary of Scotland, DIR. John Ford, co-starring Fredric March, Florence Eldridge
A Woman Rebels, DIR. Mark Sandrich, co-starring Thomas Lane, Elizabeth Allan

1937
Quality Street, DIR. George Stevens, co-starring Franchot Tone, Fay Bainter
Stage Door, DIR. Gregory La Cava, co-starring Ginger Rogers, Adolphe Menjou, Gail Patrick, Constance Collier

1938
Bringing up Baby, DIR. Howard Hawks, co-starring Cary Grant, Charles Ruggles, May Robson
Holiday, DIR. George Cukor, co-starring Cary Grant, Doris Nolan

1940
The Philadelphia Story, DIR. George Cukor, co-starring Cary Grant, James Stewart, Ruth Hussey

1942
Woman of the Year, DIR. George Stevens, co-starring Spencer Tracy, Fay Bainter

"I want you to kiss me — for luck!"

Spencer TRACY Katharine HEPBURN in WOMAN OF THE YEAR A Metro-Goldwyn-Mayer PICTURE

Left: Woman of the Year was the first and one of the best in the series of Hepburn/Tracy vehicles. The *Baltimore Sun* hailed her performance as showing 'subtlety and depth, despite the light nature of the story.'

Keeper of the Flame, DIR. George Cukor, co-starring Spencer Tracy, Richard Whorf

1943
Stage Door Canteen, DIR. Frank Borzage, Hepburn playing herself

1944
Dragon Seed, DIR. Jack Conway, Harold S Bucquet, co-starring Walter Huston, Aline MacMahon

1945
Without Love, DIR. Harold S Bucquet, co-starring Spencer Tracy, Lucille Ball

1946
Undercurrent, DIR. Vincente Minnelli, co-starring Robert Taylor, Robert Mitchum

1947
The Sea of Grass, DIR. Elia Kazan, co-starring Spencer Tracy, Melvyn Douglas
Song of Love, DIR. Clarence Brown, co-starring Paul Henreid

1948
State of the Union, DIR. Frank Capra, co-starring Spencer Tracy, Van Johnson, Angela Lansbury, Adolphe Menjou

1949
Adam's Rib, DIR. George Cukor, co-starring Spencer Tracy

1951
The African Queen, DIR. John Huston, co-starring Humphrey Bogart, Robert Morley, Peter Bull

1952
Pat and Mike, DIR. George Cukor, co-starring Spencer Tracy

1955
Summertime, DIR. David Lean, co-starring Rossano Brazzi

1956
The Rainmaker, DIR. Joseph Anthony, co-starring Burt Lancaster

The Iron Petticoat, DIR. Ralph Thomas, co-starring Bob Hope, James Robertson Justice, Robert Helpmann

1957
Desk Set, DIR. Walter Lang, co-starring Spencer Tracy, Gig Young

1959
Suddenly Last Summer, DIR. Joseph L Mankiewicz, co-starring Elizabeth Taylor, Montgomery Clift

1962
Long Day's Journey into Night, DIR. Sidney Lumet, co-starring Ralph Richardson, Jason Robards Jr

Above: A color portrait taken at about the time she met Tracy.

1967
Guess Who's Coming to Dinner, DIR. Stanley Kramer, co-starring Spencer Tracy, Sidney Poitier, Katharine Houghton

1968
The Lion in Winter, DIR. Anthony Harvey, co-starring Peter O'Toole, Jane Merrow, John Castle, Timothy Dalton, Anthony Hopkins

1969
The Madwoman of Chaillot, DIR. Bryan Forbes, co-starring Charles Boyer, Edith Evans, Margaret Leighton, Nanette Newman, Richard Chamberlain, Yul Brynner, Donald Pleasance, Danny Kaye

1971
The Trojan Women, DIR. Michael Cacoyannis, co-starring Vanessa Redgrave, Genevieve Bujold, Irene Papas

1973
A Delicate Balance, DIR. Tony Richardson, co-starring Paul Scofield, Lee Remick

1975
Rooster Cogburn, DIR. Stuart Miller, co-starring John Wayne

1978
Olly Olly Oxen Free, DIR. Richard Colla, co-starring Kevin McKenzie

1981
On Golden Pond, DIR. Mark Rydell, co-starring Henry Fonda, Jane Fonda

1985
The Ultimate Solution of Grace Quigley, DIR. Anthony Harvey, co-starring Nick Nolte

Right: Cukor directing Kate and Sir Laurence Olivier in the television film *Love Among the Ruins* (1975), the delightful story of the reunion in old age of a pair of lovers. As *Variety* noted: 'The three together have more show business experience than the Atlantic has water. The professionalism showed through.'

Index

ACKNOWLEDGMENTS

The publisher would like to thank Martin Bristow, who designed this book, Sara Dunphy for picture research, Pat Coward, the indexer, and Jessica Orebi Gann, the editor. We should also like to thank the following institutions and agencies for permission to reproduce illustrative material.

Bettmann Archive: pages 1, 5, 11 (bottom, 13 (top), 14 (bottom), 16, 22 (top), 32 (bottom), 37 (top), 40, 41, 47 (top), 49 (bottom), 57 (bottom), 60, 61, 64, 66, 78 (bottom)
Brompton Photo Library: 2, 6, 8, 11 (top), 14 (top), 15 (both), 17 (bottom), 18, 19, 22 (bottom), 31, 33, 34 (bottom), 37 (bottom), 38, 42 (both), 43, 44/45, 47 (bottom), 50, 51, 54 (bottom), 55, 58 (both), 59 (both), 63, 65, 67, 68 (bottom), 69, 70 (both), 71, 72, 74 (top), 75, 76, 77, 78 (top)
National Film Archive, London: page 52
Reuters/Bettmann; page 74 (bottom)
Springer/Bettmann Film Archive: pages 23 (bottom), 25, 28, 29 (bottom), 32 (top), 34 (top), 39, 46, 48, 56
UPI/Bettmann: pages 4, 7, 9 (both), 10, 12, 13 (bottom), 17 (top), 20, 21 (both), 23 (top), 24, 26/27, 29 (top), 30, 35, 36, 49 (top), 53, 54 (top), 57 (top), 62, 68 (top), 73